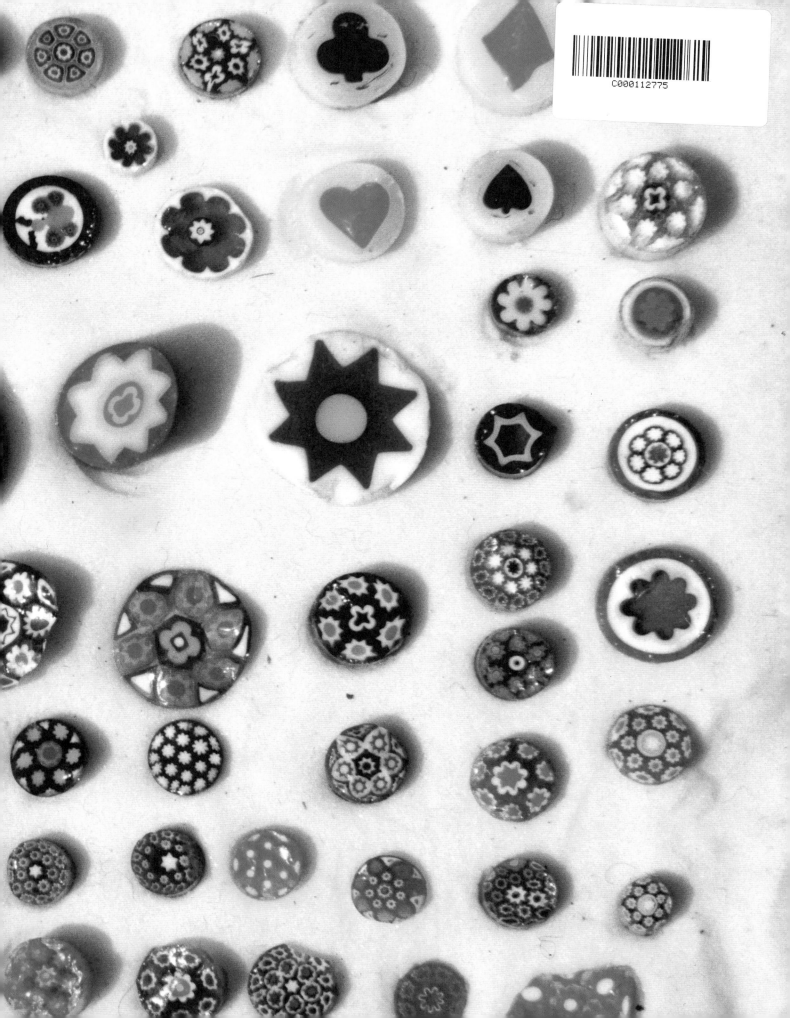

Scottish
PAPERWEIGHTS

ROBERT G. HALL

Schiffer Publishing Ltd

4880 Lower Valley Road, Atglen, PA 19310 USA

DEDICATION

For my Grandchildren, Hannah,
Sophie, Charles, and Bethany.

With Love XXXX

Library of Congress Cataloging-In-Publication Data

Hall, Robert G., 1943-
Scottish paperweights / Robert Graham Hall.
     p.   cm.
Includes bibliographical references.
ISBN 0-7643-0828-9
1. Paperweights--Scotland--Catalogs. I. Title.
NK5440.P3H35   1999
748.8'1'09411--dc21
99-19118
CIP

Designed by Bonnie M. Hensley
Layout by Randy L. Hensley
Type set in CopprplGoth BT/BernhardMod BT/ZapfHumnst BT

ISBN: 0-7643-0828-9
Printed in China
1 2 3 4

Published by Schiffer Publishing Ltd.
4880 Lower Valley Road
Atglen, PA 19310
Phone: (610) 593-1777; Fax: (610) 593-2002
E-mail: Schifferbk@aol.com
Please visit our web site catalog at **www.schifferbooks.com**

In Europe, Schiffer books are distributed by Bushwood Books
6 Marksbury Avenue Kew Gardens
Surrey TW9 4JF England
Phone: 44 (0)181 392-8585; Fax: 44 (0)181 392-9876
E-mail: Bushwd@aol.com

This book may be purchased from the publisher.
Include $3.95 for shipping. Please try your bookstore first.
We are interested in hearing from authors with book ideas on related subjects.
You may write for a free printed catalog.

Contents

ACKNOWLEDGMENTS

Many people have helped with photos and advice in the writing of this book including glass companies and individuals, and my grateful thanks goes to them collectively, but a special thanks must go to:

Roy and Pam Brown for allowing me to photograph their collection of Scottish paperweights and the help and advice given so generously.

Terry and Hilary Johnson for their hospitality and allowing me to feature their superb collection of Ysart paperweights, and the associated work conducted by Terry on the ultraviolet lamp.

Andy Barbaro who has been there when required to sort out my computer hiccups.

Joan Pettifor who dots the "i"s and crosses the "t"s in the laborious task of proofreading the book for me.

Schiffer Publishing and the talented staff, who take my large box of papers and photographs, give them a good shuffle and produce "The Book."

Many thanks to the following people who have made the task so much easier with their advice and photographs.

Anne Anderson
Caithness Glass
John Deacons
Edinburgh Crystal
Danny Fair
Mr. and Mrs. Richard Giles.
Bert and Louise Gunn
Nichola Johnson
Alistair MacIntosh
Willie Manson and Family
Peter McDougal
Anne Metcalfe
National Museums of Scotland
Perthshire Paperweights
Margaret Preston
Adele Robertson, nee Ysart
Selkirk Glass
Colin Terris

This book has certain elements that have made writing it a great deal easier because of previous research undertaken by many collectors and students of Scottish paperweights. Two people in particular, Roy Brown and Terry Johnson, have made tremendous efforts to identify who made what, when and where. Both men are keen collectors of all kinds of paperweights including antique French, modern English and American. Both are members of the Cambridge Paperweight Circle (CPC) of which Roy Brown has taken on the task of Chairman for the organization in 1998. Terry and Roy have very fine collections of Ysart paperweights, as you will see from the number of courtesy lines on the photographs in this book. The Ysart paperweights in this book are mainly based on their collections. Roy Brown is one of the leading experts in cane identification, and many collectors have benefited from his very extensive knowledge of millefiori canes, their structure, shape and coloring. Terry Johnson has taken on the task of identifying paperweights by the way in which the weights fluoresce under ultraviolet light. It is because of Terry and Hilary Johnson's large and varied collection of Ysart weights, and the meticulous way Terry has conducted his experiments, that the fluorescent method allied to a specialist knowledge of Ysart paperweights can be relied on for the unsigned Ysart attributions.

Roy Brown.

When Roy deliberates over a set of canes, "the answer is in there somewhere," he must be thinking. Over the years Roy has built up a fantastic collection of millefiori canes and lampwork from glass houses and artists worldwide, which he displays in this custom built multilevel display case. Roy and his wife Pam travel extensively to paperweight functions worldwide, and have attended several Paperweight Collector Association conventions in America, where many paperweight makers have donated canes and lampwork to his formidable collection. Roy's ambition is to have an international, representative sample from every past and present paperweight artist, or company involved in paperweights, so that they can be cataloged for future reference and research.

With the benefit of almost two hundred paperweights made by the Ysart family in Terry and Hilary's collection, Terry undertook substantial research to identify unmarked paperweights that were almost certainly made by either Salvador or Paul Ysart. He needed just one other element to make identification conclusive. Thus, the ultraviolet lamp has provided the final element of proof for attribution to certain time periods and makers.

Terry undertook a series of fluorescence testing, that kept him shut away in a pitch black room for many hours, until he made the connections that placed almost identical paperweights made by Paul Ysart into different factories and time periods. Many of Paul's most easily recognized works include his bouquets, flower posies tied with a ribbon, and butterfly weights that he made throughout his long career, and which could have been made in the 1930s or as late as the 1970s. These weights fluoresce differently depending in which glassworks they were made, and by starting with a weight known to have been made at a certain time and place, other weights which fluoresce the same can reasonably be assumed to have been made at the same place. Long established glass houses rarely changed the composition formula of the batch, as the pot of molten glass is known. Paul Ysart varied his glass only slightly during his career, but that slight difference shows up in the color the weights fluoresce. It is recognized that Terry's fluorescent method is not 100% foolproof, as certain colors and individual canes can influence the ultraviolet color, but coupled with his close examination and handling of a large quantity of Ysart weights, it will have to suffice until another more reliable method is found.

Ultraviolet light is a visible light that is emitted when a

Roy Brown's Collection of Canes and Lampwork.

With the help of Roy Brown's box of canes it was concluded that a selection of millefiori canes, held by Royal Brierley Crystal of Stourbridge, England, which were thought to have been used in their glassware many years ago, were in fact canes made by Strathearn and Vasart of Scotland, and brought to Stourbridge by visiting glassworkers on an exchange training program. Because of Roy's expertise in cane identification and the research he undertakes after acquiring a new paperweight to confirm or correct an attribution, I am certain that any weights featured in this book that are from his collection can be relied upon totally. Most of Roy's Paul Ysart paperweights that did not have a PY signature and were acquired during Paul's lifetime were photographed for Paul to identify personally. Paul did confirm most of Roy's Ysart weights, but not all, as can be seen in the chapter on fakes.

Terry Johnson.

substance within the glass is excited by an outside light with a shorter wavelength than that which is being emitted. When fluorescent tests were being carried out, it was found that to reach a conclusion, short and long wave ultraviolet light should be used. The following list is the result of Terry Johnson's tests conducted on known paperweights made by Paul Ysart at Harland, Caithness and his early years at the Moncrieff Glassworks. Salvador Ysart paperweights with a Y cane were tested and fluoresced exactly the same as early work by his son Paul, and by Frank Eisner, another paperweight maker, who all worked together at Moncrieff's in the 1930s.

	Short Wave	Long Wave
Strathearn Glass	BLUE	GREEN
Caithness Glass	BLUE	GREEN
Harland Glass	GREY	PINK-LILAC
Moncrieff Glass	GREY	GREEN
Vasart	GREY	GREEN
Fake Weights (slipped PY canes)	BLUE	GREEN

Every year a CPC member opens his or her house and paperweight collection to members of the CPC, and this year Terry and Hilary Johnson were our kind hosts. They live on the outskirts of London, and members traveled up to two hundred miles to attend the open day, which had extremely favorable weather conditions, enabling visitors to enjoy a little summer warmth and outdoor hospitality. Terry and Hilary have a fine and varied collection, and members also brought along their latest acquisitions for comment and verification by our very knowledgeable committee members. On this occasion, in excess of seventy members enjoyed the visit.

Cambridge Paperweight Meeting, August 1998.

INTRODUCTION

The Scottish glass industry, paperweight producers and the many artists who currently make paperweights, readily acknowledge the enormous contribution made to Scottish art glass by the Ysart family since their arrival in Scotland in 1921.

Salvador Ysart	1877-1955
Paul Ysart	1904-1991
Augustine Ysart	1906-1956
Vincent Ysart	1909-1971
Antoine Ysart	1911-1942

Originally from Spain, the family was recruited to Scotland because of a chronic shortage of skilled glassworkers. Salvador began working at the John Moncrieff Glassworks in Perth, where he was employed as a skilled commercial glassblower. It was not long before his skills came to the attention of the management, and in particular John Moncrieff's wife, Marriane Isobel Moncrieff, who had noticed that Salvador was making small decorative items for family and friends during his lunch breaks.

The practice of working in their own time was encouraged by the management as a way of expanding the skills of the glassmakers. Salvador was encouraged to further develop the small bowls and vases, with their distinctive colors and patterns, into a full range of items which were shown on the Moncrieff stand at the British Industries Fair in London in 1924. The range of glassware was called Monart and was well received by the quality gifts trade. By 1925, all four of Salvador's sons were working at Moncreiff's under the guidance of Salvador. The Ysart family were the only ones allowed to make Monart glass and had considerable influence with the management at this time. The family stayed together at Moncrieff's making art glass.Eventually, this developed into making paperweights, for the most part crafted by Paul.

At the outset of the Second World War in 1939, all production was turned over to the war effort, and at the end of hostilities in 1945 Moncrieff's still had a full order book for industrial glass and refused to allow Salvador to continue with his Monart production. This caused a rift in the family, and in 1946 Salvador left with two of his sons to start his own company which he named Vasart. Antoine had been killed in a road accident in 1942, and Paul stayed on at Moncrieff's. Monart production was eventually restarted by Paul, but his main passion had now become paperweights. Over the next thirty-five years Paul was a major influence on the glassmaking industry in Scotland. Wherever he worked, he was inspirational, and whoever he worked with gained a knowledge and understanding of paperweight making that would inspire several of his trainees eventually to start their own glass houses making paperweights. Among the trainees who were influenced by Paul were Peter Holmes of Selkirk Glass, Willie Manson of William Manson Paperweights, John Deacons of "J" Glass and John Deacons Paperweights, and Colin Terris of Caithness Glass. Each of these designers and makers of fine paperweights learned the secrets of glassmaking from a master craftsman and are even now taking this skillful and beautiful art form to new heights in glass artistry and design.

This book covers all the known makers and glass houses that have made paperweights from c. 1835 to the present day. Thankfully the histories of these makers are relatively well documented and all are retold within these covers.

One aspect of paperweights made in Scotland that is an issue that has not been resolved is the question of fakes. It is impossible to produce a book on Scottish paperweights without the question of the faked paperweights being brought up. Therefore, a chapter on reproductions and copies is included within this book, not I might add to point a finger, but to document an event in the history of glass in Scotland, and to try and value these pieces, which are thought to number around two thousand.

On my travels around Scotland researching the different makers, it soon became apparent that the Scottish glass industry has many connections with each other and that many glassmakers have worked with and known each other at some stage in their individual careers. This close knit family of Scottish glassmakers are now the recognized world leaders in the design and manufacture of quality glass paperweights.

About the Price Guide

The prices have been set in US dollars at $1.60 to a £1 Sterling. The price guide of a paperweight has been calculated by current auction values, and specialist dealer prices for weights, found to be in good condition. Prices rise and fall due to demand and rarity, and the author accepts no responsibility for paperweights that may sell for more or less than the values given in this book.

CHAPTER 1

MAKING A PAPERWEIGHT

There are many steps in the making of even the simplest of paperweights, and in something as special as a double overlay weight the many stages required can total thirty or so different procedures before packaging for sale and shipping. There is insufficient space to illustrate every action a master paperweight maker may take to complete his task, but I have picked out some of the basic, plus one of the more interesting procedures which may be encountered on a glass house visit.

Sometimes the colored rods are used together to make a spiral or latticinio (lace) cane, which can then be used as a bed for the millefiori canes to be set on, or used as decorative spacing between the millefiori canes. In this photograph the glassmaker has picked up three solid white canes on the end of his pontil rod, which has a small gather of clear glass attached in the first stage of making a latticinio rod, extensively used by Scottish glass houses.

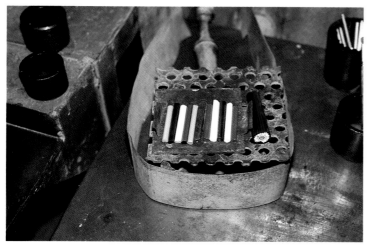

The process begins with solid rods of colored glass which can be bundled together to form a more complex cane that can be reheated to a temperature that allows the glass to become malleable and pulled out to about a quarter of an inch in diameter. The solid rods can be heated and pressed into steel molds to make interesting star and cog shapes. Once the desired shape and color has been achieved the millefiori cane, as it is now known, is cut to the length required which is usually one-eighth to one-quarter of an inch long.

The rods are carried to the workbench and pressed into a steel mold, which has an amount of hot glass already inside waiting to receive the three white rods. These rods are cooler and firmer than the almost molten clear glass and can be pushed into the glass quite easily. After a few moments to allow cooling, the glass billet can be removed from the mold.

The billet of glass is reheated at the furnace entrance to allow the glass to become malleable and to allow the white rods to reach the same temperature as the enclosing glass billet.

The length the rod can be drawn out depends on the initial size of the glass billet, in this case about fifteen feet, but in extreme cases it can be stretched to thirty or forty feet. This also reduces the size of the cane to matchstick thickness but still retains the interior design perfectly, in miniature.

The glass is then attached to a winding device which revolves the soft glass while the other end is firmly held by an assistant. This imparts a twist to the glass rod.

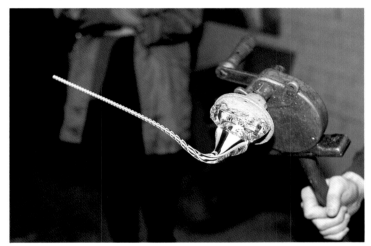

After the stretched rod has cooled and has been cut to short lengths, the remaining piece left on the winder is discarded. The twisted latticinio cane can be seen quite clearly in this photograph.

The rod is gently pulled away from the revolving winder and stretched to the desired thickness of approximately a quarter of an inch.

Many paperweights have colored bases to contrast with the millefiori canes and lampwork, which are set in or above the ground. In this illustration, a worker is collecting colored glass chippings which adhere to the hot glass, and when heated at the entrance to the furnace the colored glass fuses smoothly to form the base of the paperweight.

Millefiori canes after being cut to equal lengths are placed in steel ring molds in a set design or pattern. After the ring has been filled and packed tightly to prevent slippage, molten glass is gently lowered on to the set-up, after a few seconds to allow cooling, the canes can be lifted out of the ring for further working at the furnace

After sufficient cooling, the finished paperweight is allowed to fall gently on to a soft fireproof surface.

Back on his chair, the glassworker then proceeds to shape and polish the almost complete weight. The final shaping is done with wet newspaper held flatly in the palm of the hand. He gently shapes the dome of the paperweight. Applied pressure with strong steel pincers cuts in at the base of the weight, and starts to detach the paperweight from the pontil rod.

A gentle stream of cool air is played on the remaining glass that holds the weight to the pontil, allowing the paperweight to be broken away from the pontil rod with a sharp tap on the rod.

Immediately after being detached from the pontil rod, the finished paperweight is placed in the annealing oven to prevent cooling too rapidly, which can result in cracks appearing in the glass. This annealing process can take as long as twenty-four hours, depending on the size of the piece.

After cooling, paperweights are given a final polish to remove impurities from the surface, and overlay weights have the windows cut through the outer covering of colored glass.

Finished and unfinished overlay and millefiori paperweights awaiting final inspection before shipping.

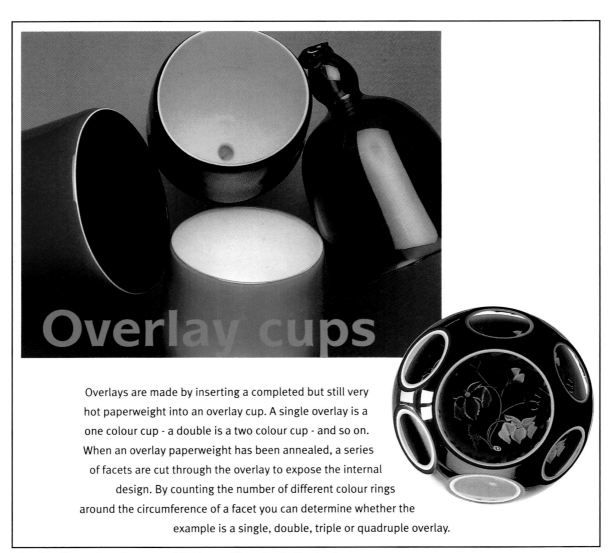

Overlays are made by inserting a completed but still very hot paperweight into an overlay cup. A single overlay is a one colour cup - a double is a two colour cup - and so on. When an overlay paperweight has been annealed, a series of facets are cut through the overlay to expose the internal design. By counting the number of different colour rings around the circumference of a facet you can determine whether the example is a single, double, triple or quadruple overlay.

Overlay Illustration. *Courtesy of Caithness Glass, Perth, Scotland.*

The techniques involved with overlaying paperweights with multicolored layers of glass has been perfected at most modern glass factories, and in this respect modern glassworks, such as Caithness, have surpassed the old masters of the 19th century, Clichy, Baccarat and others who had made paperweights in the classic period of 1845 to 1855.

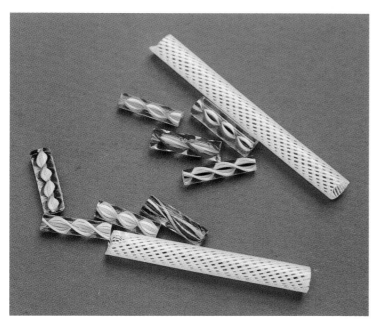

Latticinio and Filigree Canes.

Latticinio cane is made up of white cane only within clear glass, and spiral or filigree cane is usually made using single or multiple combinations of colored glass rods.

Millefiori Cane Molds. *Courtesy of Caithness Glass, Perth, Scotland.*

Many variations of molds can be used in the construction of a millefiori cane, and the three most common Daisy, Star, and Ribbed can be seen here. These molds have the initials of Paul Ysart on the sides, and were used by him during his Caithness years.

Paul Ysart. *Photo Courtesy of Adele Robertson.*

Paul Ysart setting millefiori canes into steel molds ready for the encasing process to begin. A fine selection of paperweights on show, including a Dragonfly and Butterflies. This photograph was taken around 1960.

CHAPTER 2

JOHN FORD

HOLYROOD FLINT GLASS WORKS
ESTABLISHED 1835, CLOSED 1904

Canongate, Edinburgh, Scotland

John Ford came from a family of glassworkers who had originated in the industrial Northeast of England, an area steeped in the traditions of glassmaking. The Ford family moved North to the city of Edinburgh, perhaps after seeing a business opportunity in an area that was growing in size, but did not possess a significant glassmaking facility. Whereas the Northern English area of Newcastle and nearby Yorkshire had more than enough glass houses to cope with local demand. The business started in 1812, and was known as the Caledonian Glass Works.

The firm was controlled by William Ford, John's uncle. On William's death, a new board of directors was formed which included John Ford, who in 1835 eventually became the sole owner of the business, which he renamed the Holyrood Flint Glass Works. The business flourished under John's guidance, making high quality tableware, decanters and various ornamental objects, many of which were engraved and contained the very fashionable ceramic sulphides made popular by Aspley Pellat and Josiah Wedgwood. In 1837 the glassworks were appointed Flint Glass Makers to Queen Victoria, and received several orders from the Queen for small gifts for her friends and immediate family. Small mugs and goblets were the usual gift, but it is possible that she also gave paperweights that could contain sulphide portraits of famous persons like Robbie Burns the popular Scottish poet, or perhaps of herself or her husband Albert.

In 1898 the Queen's continued patronage was recognized with a Royal Warrant and the firm became known as the Royal Holyrood Glass Works. The business made many different novelty items and from around the middle of the 19th century, paperweights would probably figure quite prominently in the company's sales catalog. Salesmen for the company traveled extensively throughout Scotland and the North of England and as far South as Derby in the English Midlands.

The men who made the sulphide medallions that were encased in the paperweights very often signed their work. Names that can be found discreetly etched into the sulphides include work by Moore, Wood, L.C. Wyon, and Andrieu. Of all the known paperweights attributed to this glassworks, none have any millefiori, lampwork or colored glass included in the design.

As with most 19th century glass houses, their paperweight making days were very brief, and as popularity declined rapidly around 1850, the company withdrew from the paperweight market with just a few being made for special occasions such as Queen Victoria's "Jubilee" in 1887. A reference to paperweights appears in "English Crystal Cameos," and is featured in *Country Life*, June 3, 1949, by Bernard G. Hughes, who says that, from about 1875, *"John Ford and Co. of Edinburgh, made exquisite crystal cameo paperweights and other items resembling that of the Apsley Pellatt glass of the 1820s, and that sulphide cameos of Queen Victoria were embedded in cube paperweights to commemorate her Jubilee of 1887."*

The company remained a substantial force in the glass business with markets found as far afield as Australia, but in 1904, the factory was closed for commercial reasons.

Robert Burns Sulphide Paperweight, John Ford. Height 3".
Courtesy of The National Museums of Scotland, Edinburgh, Scotland.

Although John Ford never used millefiori or color in his paperweights, the addition of engraving to the outside surface of the piece adds tremendous interest to these rare and historic weights. This paperweight has a beautifully carved ceramic head and shoulder view of Scotland's most famous son, the poet Robbie Burns. The detail is extremely fine and signed beneath the sulphide by the artist with the signature "Moore." The engraving on the sides of the weight are of oak leaves and acorns.

Duke of Wellington Paperweight, John Ford. Height 4".
Courtesy of The National Museums of Scotland, Edinburgh, Scotland.

This paperweight would seem to be more of an ornamental piece than a paperweight for holding down paperwork on a desk, because of its unstable and top heavy construction. Balanced on two diamond cut, tapering feet, it was probably designed to be viewed as a mantle ornament. This weight is diamond engraved on the one side with Wellington and on the other side Holyrood Glass Works.

George Herriot Sulphide Paperweight, John Ford. Height 3".
Courtesy of The National Museums of Scotland, Edinburgh, Scotland.

Fine detail can be seen in this sulphide of George Herriot, a 17th century benefactor of the poor and sick, who donated money towards charitable causes. The sulphide tablet measures only approximately 1" in height, and the magnifying properties of the crystal dome makes the subject look larger. The sulphide has been carved with such skill that the figure is easily recognizable and would have been the photographic equivalent of the day. The subject is garlanded with fine engraving of stalks, leaves and flower heads. This piece is signed under the shoulder of the subject, but the lettering is unreadable from the photograph supplied.

**William Gladstone Paperweight, John Ford. Dia. 2.25",
Height 2.75". $300/400.** *Courtesy of Mr. and Mrs. Richard
Giles.*

This paperweight is signed beneath the shoulder L.C. Wyon.
F. At the time this cast was made the subject would have
been easily recognizable to most of the current population of
Great Britain, but 150 years on this piece has caused a little
confusion by being described in my book on English Paperweights published by Schiffer Publications, as being the
English Prime Minister Disraeli, when in fact it is William
Ewart Gladstone, another English Prime Minister. The weight
has the same profile as the previous examples from this glass
house, but this piece is not engraved.

**Captain Cook/Lord Nelson Paperweight, John Ford. Dia.
2.25", Height 2.75". $300/400.** *Courtesy of Mr and Mrs.
Richard Giles.*

The engraved sulphide plaque bears a resemblance to both
Cook and Nelson, the owners of this weight have left it to
the readers to decide whichever is the correct attribution.
The subject is dressed in a jacket similar to that worn by
seafaring captains of the 18th and 19th century and should
help in identifying the subject.

Prince Albert Doorknob. $300/400. *Courtesy of Mr. and
Mrs. Richard Giles.*

This piece is unsigned and may be by John Ford, or his English
counterpart Apsley Pellat. Pellat was also making sulphide
paperweights in the early part of the 19th century.

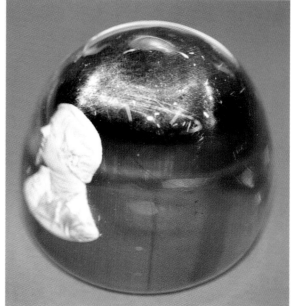

Side View of Unknown/ George Herriot Paper- weight.

A very unusual feature of the Ford sulphides is the way the plaque is set on the face of the weight, unlike the English and French sulphide makers who placed the sulphide flat to the base to be viewed from above. These paperweights are designed to be seen vertically, probably as desk or mantle ornaments. The sulphide rests on the main gather of glass with approximately a quarter of an inch of covering glass to finish off.

Unknown/George Herriot Paperweight, John Ford. Dia. 2.25", Height 2.75". $300/400. *Courtesy of Anne Anderson.*

The profile of this gentleman is very similar to the earlier sulphide of George Herriot, but this weight has features that appear to show him a little older than the other one. This weight, which is the same size as the other Ford paperweights but does not have any of the engraving, and would therefore be considerably cheaper to produce. This was probably a marketing ploy to appeal to a wider range of customers.

Unknown Gentleman, John Ford. Dia. 2.25", Height 2.75". $250/ 350. *Courtesy of Anne Anderson.*

This sulphide is made the same as previous Ford paperweights with the sulphide plaque almost to the edge of the glass dome.

Caroline Bonaparte sulphide on Wine Decanter by John Ford. Height 12". $2000/3000. *Courtesy of Anne Anderson.*

This close-up of the sulphide decoration shows the sulphide has been enclosed in a bubble of glass, which has then been collapsed by sucking out most of the air from within the bubble while still attached to the pontil rod, and then added to the side of the decanter. This was a method demonstrated and perfected by the English glassmaker Apsley Pellat in the early 19th century. John Ford and company produced many decanters and decorative pieces that rival the best from the English and French producers of the day.

CHAPTER 3

PAUL YSART, 1904-1991

Wick, Scotland

Paul Ysart is generally recognized as the finest paper-weight maker of his time. His skills were learned from his father Salvador, an immigrant glassmaker from Barcelona, Spain, who in turn had learned his trade working in France at several glass houses in the Lyon and Paris areas. At the outbreak of the first world war in 1914, Salvador brought his family to Scotland to escape the escalating terror of a war-torn Europe. Salvador's first job in Scotland was at the Leith Flint Glass Company of Perth, and after leaving school, his eldest son Paul joined his father as a glassworker. It was not until 1922, when Salvador began working for the Moncrieff glass house, that Paul was apprenticed to his father and began to learn the real secrets of the glassblower's art. And secrets they were, for traditionally glassblowers always have been reluctant to pass on skills and processes, gathered over a lifetime and jealously guarded.

Paul began his paperweight making career slowly, making the occasional frigger, after his father had been encouraged by the Moncrieff family to start experimenting with colored glass. The management noticed that Salvador, who was employed as a commercial, industrial and scientific glassblower, had made vases and other items in colored glass which demonstrated many of his artistic talents. Before long Paul was spending much of his spare time experimenting with paperweight designs and skills. Many of Paul's very early works were simple concentrics, but he was a very skilled and quick learner. He knew he could do better than these early attempts which were often filled with crudely made canes and encased in a glass with a dark tinge to it. Even though these early weights, from around the early 1930s, do not show the skills that were later to be achieved by Paul, they were still better than his father's efforts and showed ingenuity and care in the set-ups. Most of these early weights were made as friggers and given away as presents to friends and acquaintances. The making of items after hours or during lunch breaks was actively encouraged by many factory owners to enable the glassworkers to expand their skill and artistry, especially in their own time.

The colors of the canes in these early pieces are often drab, holding little promise for the future. But with the ad-vent of new colors and compounds, Paul did go on to produce vibrantly colored weights. The pinnacle he achieved was his use of the sparkling material aventurine. This material, also called goldstone, was expensive at the time and only used sparingly in his better weights. Aventurine was first used in paperweights by the Venetians around the 1840s and although reasonably common in Paul's weights, it was hardly ever used by the French makers of Baccarat, Clichy and Saint Louis, and never used by any of the English makers, ancient or modern.

During the 1930s, Salvador's other three sons began work at the Moncrieff glassworks. Having been encouraged by Mrs. Moncrieff, the wife of the owner, several years before, to experiment with colored glass vases and other items, the whole of the male Ysart family could be found working together producing the now popular glassware called Monart. So named after the first three letters in Moncrieff and the last three in Ysart.

Although Monart was produced on a production basis, it was still only treated as a sideline by the factory. As the family worked together producing Monart pieces, Paul insisted that he be allowed to continue experimenting with paperweights and the materials that could be used in them. It was during this time that Paul made his discovery that a ceramic clay pipe could be encased in glass without the piece fracturing. This led Paul to experiment with the old French techniques of sulphide paperweights, perfected by the Baccarat and Clichy factories in the 1850s. Salvador did not approve of Paul diversifying and accused him of timewasting, but Paul was adamant that he be allowed to continue the development of his paperweights.

Now that Monart glass was firmly established and selling well, the company began to add to the range of decorative items it sold. The inclusion of paperweights and millefiori inkwells gave Paul the encouragement from the company that had been lacking from his family. Paul was the star of the show, his paperweights were beginning to be collected seriously at home and abroad and were treated with the respect that so far had been given only to the antique French weights. Paul began making flowers and butterflies and also signed his weights with a PY cane.

Several of these signed weights had found their way across the Atlantic to the collection of an American named Mr. C.W.Lyon, who had shown two weights to Evangeline Bergstrom. She photographed the weights and showed them in her book *Old Glass Paperweights*. The two examples were a single butterfly weight and a weight with three smaller butterflies, within a millefiori garland of canes. Mrs. Bergstrom mistakenly thought the weights were of a French origin made by an unknown maker with the initials PY. This was a mistake that was easily understood, as Paul's weights were beginning to rival the French antiques in quality and design. The knowledgeable collector with hindsight, now finds it relatively easy to distinguish Paul's work from his 19th century French counterparts, but it was not so easy before he became the well known artist he eventually became. Paul's weights from around the 1940s were usually based on concentric rows of canes, sometimes separated by spokes of latticinio and twisted colored canes. He was also producing lampworked butterflies, insects, and two-dimensional flowers in small bunches, and in one unique piece the flowers are set in a Monart vase. The flowers were only of a simple construction and the small bunches occasionally tied with a ribbon around the posy, most were set up on a colored ground and occasionally on clear glass in a stave basket.

At the start of the Second World War in 1939, the production at the Moncrieff glassworks was turned over to the war effort. During this time, nothing but industrial and scientific glass was produced. The family were also to lose a son in 1942, when Antoine was knocked off his bicycle in an accident during the enforced nighttime blackouts and died. After the end of the war, it was decided that the family would start its own glass house, as Moncrieff's had a full order book for industrial glass which was more profitable than art glass products at this time. Paul refused to leave Moncrieff's with his remaining brothers and father. There had been a meaningful amount of discontent and acrimony within the family for a considerable time, and Paul decided that this was an opportune time to make the break and go their separate ways.

Paperweight collecting worldwide received a significant boost with the start of the Paperweight Collectors Association in America. The founding President of this association was Paul Jokelson, an enthusiastic collector and dealer, who had seen paperweights with the PY signature canes, and suspected that, as the weights were beginning to appear with increased regularity, they were indeed modern weights of a comparable quality to those antique French weights, which were so highly prized with collectors everywhere. In 1955 Jokelson managed to trace Paul to the Moncrieff Glassworks in Perth and a meeting was arranged. Paul Jokelson had a shrewd business brain and realized the potential in Paul's work. He contracted with Moncrieff's to become the sole distributor of Paul's weights in America, in order to feed a growing market of collectors. Although it would seem at first to be a contradiction that a paperweight collector of antiques should want a Paul Ysart weight in his or her col-lection, the skilled promotion by Jokelson of Paul's weights as antiques of the future and the fine workmanship and artistry displayed in these weights led to rapturous acclaim in collecting circles. As a mark of exclusivity Paul agreed that only fine collector's weights destined for America would have his PY signature cane included within the weight. He also expanded on his designs to incorporate very intricate combinations of millefiori canes. These were simple cogs and star canes bundled together and pulled down to a normal cane size, cut and then bundled together again to make extremely complex canes. His artistry with lampworked snakes, butterflies and fish were a joy to collectors everywhere and when conjoined with millefiori canes in baskets and garlands, a delight to the eye.

At the age of 61 and at the height of his fame in the paperweight world, Paul decided to leave Moncrieff's with an offer from the Caithness Glassworks at Wick to become their training officer, with sole responsibility for the training of apprentice glassworkers. Although Paul's new job meant that he did not have to make weights on a production basis, he was encouraged to produce new styles of weights in structure and design. Any weights he did make were unsigned and usually sold in the company's retail shop on site for just a few pounds. These unsigned weights carried a stick-on label on the base which read PY Made in Scotland. His very best pieces did incorporate his signature cane PY, but these pieces were becoming fewer as most were still being sent to the USA and because of time spent on his training duties. Although this area of Scotland is about as remote from the rest of the country as you can get, only 15 miles from John-O-Groats the most northerly point in the British Isles, it is on the tourist route to this well visited spot. A visit to the glass factory and shop was a must for all visitors to this part of Scotland and Paul's weights sold well.

During his years at Caithness, Paul came into contact with an expert designer named Colin Terris, who worked alongside him to develop new concepts and designs in paperweight making. Paul showed Colin Terris a range of complex millefiori canes which he had kept as reference pieces. Colin designed a range of highly decorative jewelry for men and women incorporating these canes in silver mounts. The jewelry became very fashionable and sold well. Advertising brochures of the time show a very distinguished photograph of Paul with two beautiful models displaying the jewelry which included earrings, cufflinks, rings and brooches. Paul was helped in the making of the jewelry canes by Peter Holmes.

In 1970, at aged 66 years and at time when most people are retiring, Paul left Caithness Glass to start his own glass house at an old RAF radio station building, on a remote farm called Harland near Wick. Paul's years at Harland deserve a separate chapter and are reviewed under The Harland Years.

Paul Ysart and Salvador Ysart paperweights from the Moncrieff years fluoresce in the short wave gray, and in the long wave green. All the weights in this chapter fluoresce in the same way.

Close Packed Millefiori, Paul Ysart. Dia 3.3", Height 2.3". $700/ 900. *Courtesy of Terry and Hilary Johnson.*

Paul Ysart close packed weights are quite rare and a welcome addition to any collection. The variety of canes used in these weights are a great help in identifying other weights from the same period and maker. This weight is unsigned but easily identified by the matching of canes to signed PY paperweights. Many of the canes are of a relatively simple construction, but complex canes can also be found within the weight.

Scrambled Paperweight, Paul Ysart. Dia.3.1", Height 2.3". $600/ 700. *Courtesy of Terry and Hilary Johnson.*

This paperweight comprises chippings and broken canes left at the end of a workshift. Again these pieces are quite rare from Paul Ysart and are good reference pieces as usually several whole canes can be found amongst the bits and pieces. This piece has the added attraction of a row of spaced bubbles. Paul was to use bubbles in many of his later weights, especially during his years at the Harland Glassworks.

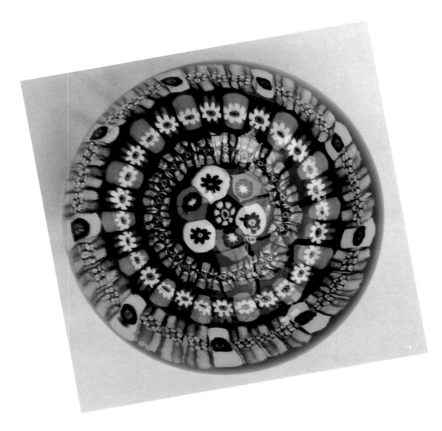

Four Row Concentric, Paul Ysart. Dia. 3.25", Height 2.75". $600/700. *Author's Collection.*

An odd combination of colors, in this early weight from Paul Ysart, with the blue and green canes not too compatible. Several of the canes bear a striking likeness to his father's canes and quite possibly were made by Salvador and used alongside more complex canes made by Paul. This weight is signed with a PY cane and has a distinctive dark smoky tinge to the covering glass. As with all paperweight makers the learning curve from quite simple weights to more complex constructions, is quite fast as the artists become confident with the materials they are using. Once the technical problems of compatibility have been overcome, the maker would have made more and more complex canes to encapsulate within the crystal dome. The vast majority of Paul and Salvador's weights were millefiori on a colored ground, and only after the concentric had been mastered did they experiment with lampwork and sulphides.

**Close Packed Millefiori, Paul Ysart. Dia.3.1", Height 2.3".
$700/900.** *Courtesy of Terry and Hilary Johnson.*

This attractive weight is set upon a pink ground. The
spaced canes are in no particular order, except that the
larger canes are set around the perimeter of the weight.
Simple cogs in many colors make up the design, with an
odd complex cane to add variety to a pretty weight.

**Patterned Paperweight, Paul Ysart. Dia. 3", Height 2.25".
$500/700.** *Courtesy of Mr. and Mrs. Richard Giles.*

This is an unusual weight from Paul Ysart, a weight made
while he worked with his father at the Moncrieff Glassworks. The very simple canes and style of the weight would
suggest a piece he made at the start of his career as a
paperweight maker.

**Garlanded Concentric with Close Packed Center, Paul Ysart.
Dia 3", Height 2.1". $700/900.** *Courtesy of Terry and Hilary
Johnson.*

This is an early example of a garlanded weight with a close
packed center. Paul Ysart in his later years, perfected this style
to a very high degree of excellence. This weight contains
mainly simple canes for the garland and close packed portion
but in a later version on the following pages, an improved
paperweight can be seen with a superior collection of canes
and presentation. The early paperweights from Paul Ysart are
highly desirable, and are eagerly contested at auction.

**Four Row Concentric, Paul Ysart. Dia. 3.2", Height 2.2". $700/
900. Courtesy** *of Terry Hilary Johnson.*

A nicely composed weight on a light blue background with special
complex canes around the outside. The white canes are made in
the pastry mold style, perfected by the French Clichy glassworks in
the 1850s, and used here with a central core of simple cog canes
which have been bundled together to form a very complex core.

Profile of Four Row Concentric, Paul Ysart.

Four Row Concentric, Paul Ysart. Dia. 3", Height 2". $400/500.
Author's Collection.

Latticinio interspaced with complex canes that are recognizable and attributable to Paul Ysart even without the PY signature cane. Probably an early weight from the late 1930s or early 1940s as the clarity of the glass dome is clearer than paperweights from very early times, when the glass had a dark tinge to the covering glass dome. Unground pontil in a slight depression.

Base of Four Row Concentric, Paul Ysart.

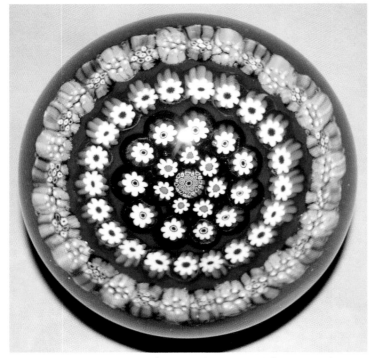

Four Row Concentric, Paul Ysart. Dia. 2.9", Height 2". $500/600.
Author's Collection.

The four rows of canes are centered on a very complex feature cane comprised of twenty four individual parts. This attractive weight is set on a royal blue ground with the pontil left unground, which does not affect the weights appearance.

Star Paperweight, Paul Ysart. Dia. 3.2", Height 2.2", $800/950.
Courtesy of Terry and Hilary Johnson.

A five-pointed star made with complex canes and set on a dark blue flashed ground makes this weight stand out from the rest. A very precise set-up with no cane slippage makes this a very desirable piece, signed with a PY cane just off the central cane.

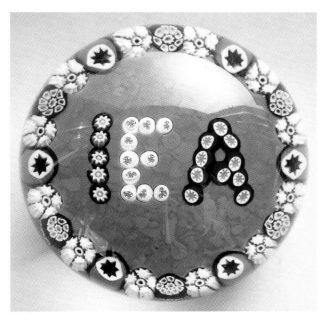

IEA Paperweight, Paul Ysart. Dia.3", Height 2.2". $500/700.
Courtesy of Terry and Hilary Johnson.

The initials IEA in this weight have still not been identified, but was probably made as a commission for a company, as several of these weights have turned up over the years. Sometimes with a different combination of canes in the garland and lettering.
The weight has a Monart label on the base, and could have been made around the time production restarted at the Moncrieff Glassworks on Monart ware, just after, or possibly even just before the Second World War. The weight is unsigned and well made with good complex canes in clear glass, and is unlikely to have been made before the late 1930s.

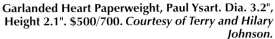

Garlanded Heart Paperweight, Paul Ysart. Dia. 3.2", Height 2.1". $500/700. *Courtesy of Terry and Hilary Johnson.*

The heart shape is composed of complex canes around a central motif cane. The heart is set on a dark ground with a garland of colorful green, orange and blue cog canes, formed to make a more complex cane, and interspersed with a green and white cane, that can be found in many of Paul's weights. This piece is unsigned.

Opposite page, bottom right:
Four Row Concentric, Paul Ysart. Dia 3.3", Height 2.2". $700/900. *Courtesy of Terry and Hilary Johnson.*

This is a nicely composed weight with good complex canes packed tightly around the central cane cluster and with the addition of a signature cane, a collector could expect to pay in excess of $1000 for such a precisely made weight.

Two IEA Paperweights, Paul Ysart. $500/700.
Courtesy of Roy Brown.

Another two IEA weights the same size as the previous weight but with different cane combinations, subtle differences, but basically the same.

Four Row Concentric, Paul Ysart. Dia. 3.1", Height 2.25". $450/600. *Courtesy of Terry and Hilary Johnson.*

Simple and complex canes all set around a green and yellow central cane. The evenly spaced set-up rests on an almost black ground. Although not signed with a signature PY cane, the canes are easily identifiable as Paul Ysart.

Bouquet Paperweight, Paul Ysart. Dia. 2.8", Height 2.1". $700/900. *Courtesy of Terry and Hilary Johnson.*

Another example with two lilac complex canes at the base of the posy. The garland of canes comprises of simple tubes and complex canes. The white tubes with the orange surround are made from a spiral cane cut to short lengths and placed in the upright position instead of the normal horizontal in which we are used to seeing them. The piece is unsigned with the base left with a slight concavity and the pontil left slightly rough.

Bouquet Paperweight, Paul Ysart. Dia. 2.8", Height 2.1". $700/900. Courtesy *of Terry and Hilary Johnson.*

This type of small posy of flowers by Paul Ysart is among the best work from this artist in glass. A simple bunch of five, six or seven stylistic flowers, buds and leaves but enough color and interest to keep the Ysart collector in a seventh heaven. The posy can be surrounded, as this one is, with a garland of millefiori canes or just left lying on a colored ground, signed or unsigned, this paperweight style is unmistakably Paul Ysart's. This is one of his early pieces judging by the pastel and simple canes in the garland. A precious paperweight and a delight to hold and examine.

Bouquet Paperweight, Paul Ysart. Dia. 2.8", Height 2.1". $800/ 1000. *Author's Collection.*

Five flowers and two buds, backed by five long broad leaves with the posy tied with a blue ribbon, makes this a delightful weight. Set upon a black ground for a dramatic contrast. This is my personal favorite among my Paul Ysart weights. This glass has a slightly oily feel, and on many occasions I have cleaned the weight in soapy water, thinking I had picked it up with greasy fingers. The glass also has a very slight dark tinge when held against a light background. These bouquet weights were all probably made when Paul worked at Moncrieff Glassworks, from the 1930s to the 1950s. This weight is unsigned.

Jasper Bouquet Paperweight, Paul Ysart. Archive Photo. $800/1000. *Courtesy of Anne Metcalfe, Sweetbriar Gallery, Helsby, England.*

The dark blue and white spattered background to this weight makes it rare and desirable to Paul Ysart collectors. The large red aventurine flower with a stardust center is also unusual and perfectly executed with skill. It is an unusual focal point to the bouquet which has the PY signature cane in the head of the pale blue flower.

Base of Bouquet Paperweight, Paul Ysart.

The pontil on this weight has been removed by cracking off the paperweight from the end of the pontil rod by sharply tapping the pontil rod once the weight has cooled sufficiently. The paperweight is allowed to fall gently onto a soft fireproof surface and then carried to the annealing ovens. After cooling, the paperweights are inspected for rough pontil scars, and in this case, because the mark has broken close to the base of the weight, it has been allowed to pass without grinding. If the pontil had protruded at all, then a light touch on a grindstone would remove the surplus glass.

**Sulphide Paperweight, Paul Ysart. Dia. 2.75", Height 2".
$600/800. *Courtesy of Terry and Hilary Johnson.***

After discovering that white clay used in the manufacture of
smoking pipes was compatible with glass, and would not
cause annealing cracks, Paul set about making castings to
be included in his paperweights. Using plastic brooches
from the local Woolworth store, he made small castings
and hand painted them with material purchased from a
Stoke on Trent pottery. This paperweight with an amber
ground, shows the original brooch from which the casting
was made. Although no great work of art, it led Paul to
greater challenges. He strived to emulate the French master
paperweight makers from Baccarat and Clichy, artisans of a
bygone age. He was undaunted in his continuing search to
unravel the mysteries still surrounding the manufacture of
paperweights.

**Sulphide Paperweight, Paul Ysart. Dia. 2.75", Height 2.75". $600/
800. *Courtesy of Terry and Hilary Johnson.***

A basket of flowers with star canes on a strawberry red ground.
Historically important as the first attempt by a Scottish glass house to
recreate sulphide paperweights in the tradition of the Holyrood
Glassworks and John Ford & Co. from the 19th century.

**Eagle Sulphide Paperweight, Paul Ysart. Dia. 3.5", Height 2.5".
$1200/1500. *Courtesy of Terry and Hilary Johnson.***

A rare sulphide of an eagle on a dark ground with a red and white
torsade. Paul Ysart made very few sulphide paperweights, even
though he had perfected the techniques by the time this weight
was produced. Paul liked the challenge of perfecting the styles of
the 19th century paperweight makers of the Classic Period (1845-
55), and once he had mastered the technique, he moved on to
answer other questions in his quest for excellence. It was not just
the ceramic sulphide that was difficult to produce but the torsade is
an extremely difficult and time consuming cane to make and insert
into a weight, which is why so few contemporary weights include
one. The very tightly wound torsade in this weight is almost
perfectly made, and a credit to the maker. The weight is discreetly
signed beneath with a PY cane.

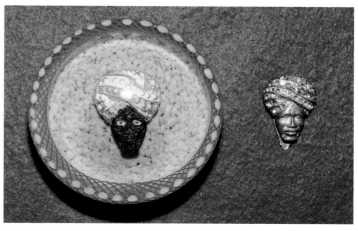

Arabian Knight Sulphide Paperweight, Paul Ysart, Archive Photo, $1000/1200. *Courtesy of Anne Metcalfe, Sweetbriar Gallery, Helsby, England.*

An Arabian Knight brooch, encrusted with gems can be seen in fine detail, but in the casting process has lost some of its sharpness. Still a fine likeness which has the added attraction of a yellow spotted torsade of red spiral glass. The yellow dots appear to be lying on the surface of the torsade, which was a technique used by Paul in later years on his snake weights.

Sulphides of King George VI and Queen Elizabeth, Paul Ysart. Archive Photo $1300/1500. *Courtesy of Anne Metcalfe, Sweetbriar Gallery, Helsby, England.*

A side-by-side profile of the reigning Monarchs of England, in the late 1930s, at the time this piece was made at the Moncrieff Glassworks. The weight was purchased directly from Paul Ysart and came with the original presentation box and brooch from which the sulphide was cast. The sulphide rests on a mottled purple ground.

Opposite page, bottom right:
Horse's Head Sulphide Paperweight, Paul Ysart. Dia. 3.25", Height 2.3". $1200/1500. *Courtesy of Terry and Hilary Johnson .*

A row of complex red and green canes make a garland around the sulphide plaque with a PY cane slipped in between the canes, at the bottom of the design. A striking contrast of color between the pure white sulphide and the black ground on which it rests. A rare and beautiful paperweight in a style perfected by the French 19th century glassworks of Clichy, but because of the rarity of Paul's sulphide weights, this weight commands a price almost double that of his antique 19th century counterparts.

Greek Goddess Sulphide Paperweight, Paul Ysart. Archive Photo. $1600/1800. *Courtesy of Anne Metcalfe, Sweetbriar Gallery, Helsby, England.*

A stunning Greek Goddess sulphide, colored in the Wedgwood style with the original cameo brooch from which it was cast. Clearly signed in the outer garland of stardust canes with a yellow center, the weight is also signed on the rear of the casting. This and other paperweights with the original brooches were purchased directly from Paul Ysart in his later years from his own collection of samples. In some cases these weights may be unique one-of-a-kind samples. This weight which is set on crystal clear glass is stunningly simple in construction, but a masterpiece of imagination.

Dragonfly and Butterflies Paperweight, Paul Ysart. Dia. 2.75", Height 2.1". $1200/1500. *Courtesy of Terry and Hilary Johnson.*

Two butterflies flank the yellow spotted dragonfly in this paperweight, which is garlanded with a row of red and green complex canes. The weight is signed with a PY cane beneath the weight. It is interesting to note the sharp increase in prices of Paul Ysart paperweights. At a recent Christie's, London sale, on 16th October 1997, a similar weight of two butterflies and a dragonfly realized a hammer price of £750 plus commission or approximately $1400. The prices realized also came as a surprise to the auctioneers. With a general guide price around $200/300 for most weights including the butterflies and salamanders, the collectors and dealers were out in force, hoping for a bargain buy. But, with a packed salesroom, prices were driven upwards to new highs for Ysart paperweights.

Butterfly Paperweight, Paul Ysart. Dia. 3.1", Height 2.25". $800/1000. *Courtesy of Terry and Hilary Johnson.*

A lovely butterfly hovers over a mottled red ground of powdered glass with a garland of pastel blue and yellow canes. The coat of mottled, powdered red glass used for the ground is the same as that used in the overlay attributed to Paul Ysart in this chapter. The rear wings of the insect are stretched and flattened canes, the same as in the outer garland. The weight is unsigned with a slight concavity to the base and with a rough pontil mark.

Pansy Paperweight, Paul Ysart. Dia. 2.7", Height 2.1". $1500/1750. *Courtesy of Terry and Hilary Johnson.*

This is the first Paul Ysart pansy I have ever seen and may be unique. It was bought from the Christie's sale of the first part of the Parkington Collection of Glass in 1997 by the present owner. Described by the auctioneer as an early Paul Ysart to which I would readily agree. It is clear that, even at this early stage in his career, Paul had equaled the best from the French 19th century makers of paperweights. The weight has a slight concavity and with the pontil lightly touched on a grinding wheel.

Overlay Paperweight, Paul Ysart. Dia. 3", Height 2.1". $800/900. *Author's Collection.*

It is very unusual to find a Paul Ysart overlay paperweight, and most collectors have never seen one, but after careful consideration I am attributing this almost unique overlay to Paul Ysart for the following reasons. The green and white canes on the outer edge, and the yellow canes can be matched to canes in signed Paul Ysart concentrics, and it is known that while at Caithness Glass between 1965 and 1970, Paul did try to make an overlay. Colin Terris the Chief Designer at Caithness has a blue Moonflower paperweight which is overlayed with blue glass chippings. In issue 10 of *Reflections*, the Caithness annual review magazine, Colin explains that the *"overlay moonflower is a very early piece dating from around 1970, and was the nearest we came to a successful overlay in those early years. We did not have the skills to make an overlay cup [see Glossary] so we coated the surface of the weight with two or three layers of chipped blue color. When faceted the result was close to a genuine overlay but we never succeeded in getting rid of the ragged edging around the circumference of the facets."* The use of chippings for the overlay leaves the surface with an orange peel effect and ragged edges to the facets, the same as in this red example. It would be reasonable to assume that, at some stage during Paul's early years, he could have tried this method, which is simple to apply and only needs the soft glass to be pushed or rolled into the glass chippings and then reheated at the furnace entrance. This would have been done several times to achieve the depth of color required.

Four-Leaf Clover Paperweight, Paul Ysart. Dia. 3.2", Height 2.25". $450/550. *Author's Collection.*

This is an unusual paperweight that would appear to have been made as a commission for a commercial customer. The base is acid etched with "TOMEY BIRMINGHAM" with the lettering arranged in a circle around the pontil mark which has been lightly touched on the grinding wheel. The clover leaf is well made, using aventurine for the leaves and light brown and olive-colored glass chippings for the mottled ground. A fake version of this piece appears in the chapter on fakes and was shown to Paul Ysart, who promptly denied making it.

Two Row Concentric Millefiori Paperweight, Paul Ysart. Dia. 2.9", Height 2". $700/900. *Author's Collection.*

An unsigned paperweight by Paul Ysart that may have been made towards the end of his career judging by the superb quality of this piece. The use of aventurine inside the spiral dividing canes makes the weight come alive with its sparkle. The canes are all pressed into the sand colored ground and are left flush with the ground. The base is almost flat with the pontil snapped off and left unground.

Faceted Concentric Millefiori Paperweight, Paul Ysart. Dia. 3.1", Height 2.1". $600/700. *Author's Collection.*

Eight large facets are cut from the center of the weight to just above the base to add something a little different to this already lovely weight. The orange spiral cane with a yellow core is set flush into the royal blue ground to make a stunning contrast. The second row of canes from the center is a combination of complex yellow and purple canes, interspersed with short lengths of white spiral canes which have been stood on end for variety.

Concentric Paperweight, Paul Ysart. Dia. 3.25".Height 2.3". $450/ 600. *Author's Collection.*

Strong coloring of the orange and green rods, laid as spacing canes between the simple cogs and star canes makes this an attractive weight. Set on a dark ground for added effect, the paperweight is nice but has no special qualities. The weight is unsigned with a rough pontil scar.

Base of Closepacked Paperweight with Garland, Paul Ysart.

The base on this weight has been ground completely flat, which could eventually lead to scratches appearing on the base and spoiling the view. The 19th century glassworkers, with the exception of Bohemia, always left the base with a slight concavity and a small basal rim for the weight to rest upon. Thus avoiding the base getting marked with scratches.During Paul Ysart's working career, he used most of the different base finishes that can be applied to a paperweight.

Closepacked and Garlanded Paperweight, Paul Ysart. Dia. 2.75", Height 2". $800/1000. *Author's Collection.*

Dark blue and lilac complex canes makes a lovely garland around the well made close packed canes. The central canes are complex with a few simple canes mixed in. The pastel colored eggshell blue and gray canes look reminiscent of canes used by Paul's father Salvador. A closepack, such as this piece, is extremely useful in identification purposes, a problem American collectors usually do not have. Most of Paul Ysart's paperweights were sold in the USA, and all were signed with a PY cane, except for a few migratory stragglers.

With the inclusion of Paul Ysart paperweights in this book, owned by Roy and Pam Brown, means that the attribution of the following weights can be guaranteed, even without a PY cane. For each Ysart-type weight purchased, Roy Brown would send a photograph to Paul Ysart directly, who would identify and authenticate each paperweight he had made and would sign the back of the photograph sent to him. Not all photographs came back with Paul's authenticating signature. In a series of letters written by Roy and replied to by Paul's daughter Adele, on behalf of her father, it became clear that Paul could pick out paperweights that contained canes made by himself, which were used in paperweights that were definitely not made by him. Paul says in one letter dated November 1986 that, of three photographs sent to him, two were genuine and one was not made by him, although it contained his canes. In a further letter dated March 1987 to Roy, Adele says on behalf of Paul, *"without saying too much, I can only say that at some time, some of father's canes were misappropriated by another glassworker and subsequently incorporated in his weights"*

It was around 1988 that these weights began to appear on the collecting market, and were eagerly bought by an unsuspecting collecting public and dealers. It is a pity that Paul Ysart was not asked at this time to look at and identify weights with his signature cane that were supposedly fake. Also mentioned in this correspondence with Paul Ysart, Roy asks if it is possible to date some of the designs in the photographs, to which Paul replies that it is near impossible as he has made so many weights over his long career.

Typical Base of Early Paul Ysart Paperweights. *Courtesy of Pam and Roy Brown.*

This base shows a rough and unground pontil mark usually found on the base of Paul Ysart's early work. Occasionally one can be found with the pontil removed by light grinding. This was only necessary when the broken pontil was left protruding to leave the weight pivoting on the scar.

Concentric Paperweight, Paul Ysart. Dia. 3.2", Height 2.2". $600/800. *Courtesy of Pam and Roy Brown.*

An early weight made with a preciseness that was to become Paul Ysart's trademark throughout his career, and although this paperweight contains only simple canes, the coloring and composure makes it desirable and appreciated.

Butterfly Paperweight, Paul Ysart. Dia 3.1", Height 2.1". $1000/1200. *Courtesy of Pam and Roy Brown.*

Flying over clear glass, this butterfly with a blue body and green wings with yellow and orange spots, is one of the most sought after of Paul Ysart's work. Rarely appearing on the market, the weights are hotly contested at auction. A similar butterfly weight recently sold in the second part of the Parkington collection at Christie's, London, for $1100.

Paperweight with Garland, Paul Ysart. Dia 3", Height 2.2". $700/ 800. *Courtesy of Pam and Roy Brown.*

Powder blue and white canes surround a pale blue flower with leaves and stalk. The weight is unsigned and from the 1930s.

Concentric Paperweight, Paul Ysart. Dia. 3.2", Height, 2.2". $800/ 1000. *Courtesy of Pam and Roy Brown.*

A stunning weight which has a base of milk white glass between the canes. This lovely background can also be found as the base in Paul Ysart inkwells. The use of this white glass sets off the colorful spiral and simple millefiori canes to perfection. An unsigned weight, but authenticated by Paul Ysart.

Gift Paperweight, Paul Ysart. Dia. 3.1", Height 2". $700/800. *Courtesy of Pam and Roy Brown.*

This paperweight was probably made as a gift for a friend or acquaintance. The letter B is neatly composed and made from twisted pink and white glass the same as is used in Paul's bouquet weights. The weight is signed with a complexly made PY cane at the bottom.

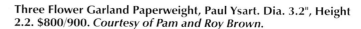

Three Flower Garland Paperweight, Paul Ysart. Dia. 3.2", Height 2.2. $800/900. *Courtesy of Pam and Roy Brown.*

Three clematis-type flowers with leaves and stalks are garlanded with complex lilac and white and red and white canes. The set-up rests on a black ground with a further three spaced complex orange canes.

Clematis with Garland Paperweight, Paul Ysart. Dia. 3", Height 2.1". $1000/1200. *Courtesy of Pam and Roy Brown.*

The striped pink body of this insect has two green and two blue wings attached, which are made from slightly flattened ordinary millefiori canes. The garland comprises spiral twists of cane with gold aventurine within. These spirals act as spacers between very complex canes, made from simple tubes in green, pink, yellow and blue, bound together to make a single composite cane.

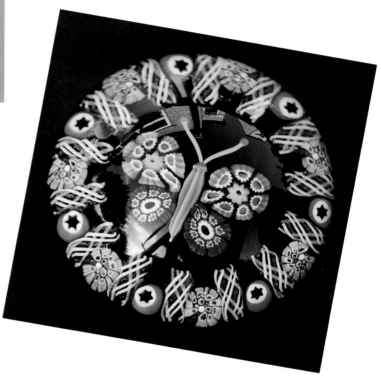

Clematis with Garland Paperweight, Paul Ysart. Dia. 3", Height 2.1". $600/700. *Courtesy of Pam and Roy Brown.*

A nice arrangement of colorful canes surround a simply made clematis type flower with striped petals.

Posy and Flower Paperweight, Paul Ysart. Dia. 2.9". Height 2". $1100/1200. *Courtesy of Pam and Roy Brown.*

A superb posy weight with a striped clematis type flower as an added bonus in this beautifully made paperweight. The signature PY can be found within the white small flower. The use of green lengths of cane in the basket, placed next to latticinio canes, was inspirational and sets this weight among Paul's best work. This weight was probably made around the 1940s and was far ahead of any other paperweight maker in design and meticulous construction. The basket is extremely difficult to achieve without distortion, and many modern glassworkers from Scotland have tried this method and only succeeded after much trial and error.

Posy and Flower Paperweight, Paul Ysart. Dia. 3", Height 2.2". $1200/1400. *Courtesy of Pam and Roy Brown.*

This weight has fourteen small flowers and a large clematis with a complex millefiori center which makes this an extra special piece. The latticinio canes in white and yellow twists form a crown for the bouquet of flowers to rest on. Meticulously executed, the paperweight is signed PY in a flowerhead center to make this weight a collector's dream.

Concentric Paperweight, Paul Ysart. Dia. 2.9", Height 2". $700/900. *Courtesy of Pam and Roy Brown.*

Aventurine twists in the outside row divide the simple green and white canes in a typical Paul Ysart paperweight. Probably the most common of all his creations, but very collectible.

Spaced Millefiori Paperweight, Paul Ysart. Dia. 3", Height 2". $800/1000. *Courtesy of Pam and Roy Brown.*

This spaced example contains complex canes that Paul Ysart called stones. After pulling a simple rod and then bundling the cut short lengths together, the now complex cane is reheated and a further pull miniaturizes the cane to the size where a strong magnifying glass is needed to see the individual segments. The finished cane may contain as many as a hundred individual parts. Paul kept as reference pieces any cane that had been made in this way and had quite a collection. The centers of several canes within these fine examples have stones incorporated within the already complex canes.

Early Inkwell, Paul Ysart. Height 5". $800/900. *Courtesy of Margaret Preston.*

This inkwell fluoresces in the same way as Paul Ysart's early paperweights from the 1930s, and was possibly one of his earliest attempts at an inkwell. Precisely set canes in three concentric circles set around a complex red and blue cane. The stopper and neck of the inkwell are made from spattered glass chippings. The whole piece is made in clear glass with the base lightly ground to remove the pontil mark. The central complex cane is typical of the canes used by Paul.

Paul Ysart's "Stones." *Courtesy of Pam and Roy Brown.*

This is a selection of canes used by Paul, which can be found in many of his weights. The three on the top row have approximately one hundred individual segments in each cane, and look like miniature close packed paperweights.

Inkwell, Paul Ysart. Height 5.25". $1400/1600 *Courtesy of Anne Metcalfe, Sweetbriar Gallery, Helsby, England.*

Signed with a PY cane, this lovely inkwell features a bouquet of flowers set on a sand-colored ground with a garland of red and complex blue canes. The stopper has three simple flowers set within a garland of millefiori canes to match the base. The bouquet of flowers in this style is reminiscent of Paul's weights from his time at Moncrieff's in the early 1930s and to show this degree of skill and artistry, at such an early time in his career, is testimony to his artistic talent.

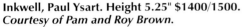

Inkwell, Paul Ysart. Height 5.25" $1400/1500. *Courtesy of Pam and Roy Brown.*

This inkwell has many simple and complex canes set very low in the base on a white ground. The thickness of the ground and canes is less than .75", relying on the magnifying properties of the glass dome to fill out the inkwell. The canes come out to the edge of the inkwell and are set in a random style. Other inkwells made by Paul can contain stylized fish and single flowers within a garland of millefiori canes.

Inkwell, Paul Ysart. Height 5.25", $1400/1500. *Courtesy of Anne Metcalfe, Sweetbriar Gallery, Helsby, England.*

A truly beautiful combination of color and construction; a complex row of canes makes a fine garland as a bonus. The deep blue petals of this double layered flower set on a bright orange spattered ground make this inkwell one of Paul Ysart's most striking creations. The piece is signed with a PY cane, but even without a signature cane the style and construction are easily recognized as by Paul Ysart.

Inkwell, Paul Ysart. Height 5.25". $ 1400/1600 *Courtesy of Anne Metcalfe, "Sweetbriar Gallery," Helsby, England.*

A wonderful selection of simple and complex canes to view within this lovely inkwell. The outer row of cog canes hold the jumble of closepacked canes together in organized chaos. The stopper mirrors the base perfectly.

Inkwell, Salvador Ysart. Height 4.3". $800/ 1200. *Courtesy of Anne Metcalfe, Sweetbriar Gallery, Helbsy, England.*

As a contrast to Paul's inkwells, this example by his father Salvador highlights the striking differences between their work. This particular inkwell was identified by Paul, who said, *"Oh yes, thats my dad's work."*

Spitfire Paperweight, Unknown Maker. Dia. 4", Height 1.6". *Courtesy of Pam and Roy Brown.*

This paperweight was shown to Paul Ysart who said he never made it, but that he had made the lampworked spitfire in the late 1930s as buttonholes for the boys, who wore them to show support for the RAF. pilots during the war. Coincidentally, I had already seen this same spitfire encased in a paperweight that is illustrated in my book *Old English Paperweights*. It belonged to Gilbert Hill a former sales director of Royal Brierley Crystal, Stourbridge, England, which is an old established glass house that has a history which goes back to the 18th century and was formerly known as Stevens and Williams. He bought the paperweight from the Job table, which was a table set up at the end of every week to sell off to the workforce any slight seconds or unwanted pieces of glass. Royal Brierley Crystal had a working relationship with Caithness Glass and Strathearn Glassworks. Several glassworkers had been seconded to Royal Brierley from Strathearn and Caithness to learn new glassworking techniques and had brought with them from Scotland a selection of canes, etc. The spitfire must have been among the canes and, eventually, inserted in a paperweight at Royal Brierley Crystal. This spitfire is identical to the Gilbert Hill piece, even to the body of the aeroplane, which has a twist imparted down its body length.

Ysart Inkwells. *Courtesy of Anne Metcalfe, Sweetbriar Gallery, Helsby, England.*

When the inkwells are placed side by side, the Salvador piece in the center has major differences in construction and cannot be confused with Paul's work. Although Salvador's work is now in much demand among collectors and is setting new highs at auction, his always falls behind the craft of his son Paul. The differences between the two men's work is obvious to all.

**Thistle Paperweight, Paul Ysart. Dia. 3" Height 2.2".
$600/800.** *Courtesy of Margaret Preston.*

This patriotic symbol of Scotland is signed at the bottom
with a complex "PY" cane in red on white. The thistle is
well constructed from green complex canes, with the
flower head made in similar purple canes and then set on a
black background.

**Footed Encased Military Cap Badge, Paul Ysart. Dia. 2.75", Height
3.75". $400/600.** *Courtesy of Margaret Preston.*

A rare and unusual table or mantel ornament, which has a regimental
cap badge encased within it. Paul Ysart was known to have made these
as keepsakes for Canadian troops stationed near Perth in the late 1930s.
The piece fluoresces identically to his early paperweights. This was not a
production item, and may have been an experiment to see which
materials could be encased, without causing the glass to fracture. Several
of these encased badges have been recorded over the years. A similar
example and other badges can be seen in Dave Webber's article for the
1998 Paperweight Collectors Association Annual Bulletin. The crown has
the words CANADA on a scroll beneath, and measures 1.5" high by
1.25" wide.

Paul Ysart at Work. *Photo Courtesy of Adele Robertson.*

Paul makes air bubbles with a steel rod by pushing it into the soft glass, air trapped inside expands to form a silver decorative bubble when reheated at the glory-hole.

Paul Ysart at Work. *Photo Courtesy of Adele Robertson*

Paul Ysart shaping the weight.

A Fine Selection. *Photo Courtesy of Adele Robertson*

Paul proudly displays a variety of paperweights made at the Harland glassworks.

CHAPTER 4

Ysart Brothers Glass, Vasart, 1946-1956

Shore Road, Perth, Scotland

The Ysart family were all in the employment of the Moncrieff Glassworks in Perth. With the outbreak of hostilities, essential war work was the order of the day and the making of art glass had to cease for the duration of the war. At the end of the Second World War, Salvador Ysart wanted to continue making the art glass he had been producing before 1939.

Under the brand name "Monart," Moncrieff's had been selling all they could make using the Ysart family to produce, design and expand this range of products. It was understandable that the Ysarts should wish to continue with this winning line, but Moncrieff's had a full order book for industrial glasswork and insufficient skilled labor to meet demand. Governmental policy of the day was to bring the country back up to full production as soon as possible, and art glass was of little interest to industrialists of the day. On refusal by Moncrieff's to restart production, Salvador decided to leave with two of his sons. His eldest son, Paul, refused to leave with his father and brothers because of a family disagreement going back many years, and Antoine had been killed in a road accident in 1942.

The glass produced in the Ysarts new venture was named Vasart which was formed by using the first letter of each Christian name of the family member working at the new glassworks, Vincent, Augustine and Salvador, with **ART** coming from the last three letters in their surname, which when conjoined produced **Vasart**.

The main production during the ten years this art glass factory was run by the Ysart family was bowls, vases and various other pieces of table and decorative ware. Paperweights were also produced in small quantities and were probably made by all the family at some time and, although not of the same quality as Paul Ysart's, they were readily acceptable to the gift trades. Although only produced as a sideline to the company's main activities, several people were kept busy setting up the canes into ring molds ready for the Ysart men and another worker, Jack Allen, to encase in a glass dome. Among the women who assembled these canes were Catherine Ysart, Vincent's wife and Pat Allen, Jack's wife. The exact quantities that were produced is not known, but

judging from the output of similar sized companies and knowing the amount of people involved in the actual production, a reasonable guess would be 100 to 150 per week. Many of the weights produced around this time are quite crude in their execution, but occasionally weights appear that show skill, thought and ingenuity.

Among the other things made with millefiori canes were car gear-stick knobs, ashtrays, door handles and cork screws. Another most successful of these items was the inkwell with matching stopper. All these show a degree of skill that could only come after many years in the glass business and were almost certainly made by Salvador Ysart alone. Most vases and other types of glassware were signed with a black and silver label on the base, but the exception were paperweights; very few can be found that identify the weight positively with a label remaining stuck on the base. In a few very rare paperweights, the initial Y for Ysart can be seen, usually around the outside edge. Identification usually means a search to match canes in known weights before attribution can be relied upon.

Business was buoyant in the early years of this family venture, but in 1955 Salvador Ysart died and only a year later Augustine died at only 48 years of age. Vincent Ysart did not relish the prospect of continuing on alone and welcomed an approach by George Dunlop, who had been a customer of the firm and who helped market the glass and paperweights through his own company Pirelli Glass, Ltd, of London. He also gave the Ysart brothers reciprocal business in the form of blank glass, which the Ysarts decorated.

A new company was started in 1956 called Vasart Glass Ltd, which prospered for several years, making paperweights and art glass, and in 1960 a manager was brought in to control the company. This man was Stuart Drysdale, a local man who was a lawyer by profession but who wanted a change of occupation. A major breakthrough in the fortunes of the company came about due to a virtual mistake. In 1963 a Teacher's Whisky bottle had been left too long in a potter's oven, which resulted in the bottle collapsing almost flat, this bottle with the Teacher's label attached was then presented to a Teacher's Whisky executive as a joke present. The executive, Mr. A.K. Bergius, realized the potential as an ash tray and advertising aid and promptly sought a glass producer to reproduce the flattened bottle in quantity. The task was eventually presented to Vincent Ysart, who after a short while produced the ashtray. At the peak of production, Vasart Glass could only make 500 ashtrays per month. This production quantity was not sufficient for the whisky giant. William Teacher's & Sons, Ltd, realized that production could not be increased by this very small glass house, which was already at 100 percent capacity with its commitments to the gifts trade with paperweights, etc. The only alternative was a new factory to cater to William Teacher's full requirements. Teacher's bought out Vasart Glass and opened a new factory in Crieff in 1965. This custom-built unit was managed by Stuart Drysdale with Vincent Ysart as works manager. It was named Strathearn Glass. Most of the workers from the Vasart company also transferred the few miles from Perth to the small town of Crieff.

Teacher's Whisky Ashtray, Vasart. $10. *Author's Collection.*

Assorted Vasart Canes. *Courtesy of Roy and Pam Brown.*

A collection of Vasart canes including simple and complex examples with two butterfly canes that are occasionally found in Salvador's paperweights.

Spaced Concentric, Vasart. Dia. 3" Height 1.6". $60/80. *Author's Collection.*

This must have been one of the very early pieces from Vasart, made around 1946 judging by the very crude canes and amount of annealing fractures around the central canes. The fracturing is the result of incompatibility between the canes and surrounding glass when glass from a different formula is mixed with another. The canes in the center of the weight are probably the most untidy examples the author has ever seen. The canes also have a dead, matte appearance to them. The weight has the typical rough ground pontil mark associated with many of the paperweights and related items from the early Vasart days. The glass used for this weight has a slight yellowish tinge to it.

Concentric Paperweight, Vasart. Dia. 2.9" Height 1.75". $80/100. *Courtesy of Terry and Hilary Johnson.*

A very early example from Vasart, displaying cog type canes with segments of spiral cane to break up the pattern of black and white, and blue and white canes.

Above: **Pin or Ash Tray, Vasart. Dia. 4", Height 1.5". $80/90.** *Author's Collection.*

The crude canes again let this nicely made ashtray down. The color combinations on the outside work are fine, but the center feature area is awash with many different odd canes. As the central feature of any millefiori object, paperweight or otherwise, the center of the piece should be the most attractive area to view, in this case it is the opposite.

Left: **Concentric Paperweight, Vasart. Dia. 3" Height 1.6" $80/100.** *Author's Collection.*

A slightly more valuable weight than the previous example as the canes fit together a little better. The glass used for the canes is the same as the glass of the encasing dome as no fracturing has occurred. This glass also has a dark gray tinge, reminiscent of early Paul Ysart paperweights from the 1930s.

Base of Ashtray.

The base of this ashtray shows the pontil removed by grinding on an abrasive wheel.

Concentric Paperweight, Vasart. Dia. 3". Height 1.75". $200/250. *Author's Collection.*

The quality is beginning to improve with the canes tightly packed together to prevent slippage and a good selection of canes. Probably made by Salvador Ysart in the late 1940s.

Three Dimensional Paperweight, Vasart. Dia. 3.5", Height 2.25" $300/400. *Author's Collection.*

This flower and leaf weight with a garland of well made canes is almost certainly by Salvador Ysart. A high degree of skill is necessary to achieve this quite complex process. Two different colors of ground are used, pink on the base and pale green in the center, from which the two levels of leaves and yellow flowers emerge. The flower is centered with a large bubble. The outer row of canes are very complex and well constructed when compared to the previous examples, and on the inside of the garland is a bed of spattered glass and then the piece is encased in a large dome of darkly tinted glass. The pontil has been removed by grinding.

Side view of the previous Vasart Concentric Paperweight.

The canes in this weight reach nearly to the top of the dome with only a quarter of an inch gap between canes and top, making the weight appear completely full to capacity. The whole set-up sits upon a bed of colored glass chippings with the pontil removed by grinding.

**Signed Concentric Paperweight, Salvador Ysart. Dia. 3",
Height 1.9". $800/1000. *Courtesy of Terry and Hilary
Johnson.***

A Y cane signed on the left side of the weight, identifies it
as being made by Salvador Ysart. Salvador's signature
cane has only been found on a dozen or so paperweights.
He must have thought that the quality of this piece
deserved to be recognized as his work, but the reason
why he signed this piece and not the rest of his quality
pieces will remain a mystery.

**Base of Previous Concentric, Salvador
Ysart.**

The pontil mark has been removed by
light grinding.

**Four Row Concentric, Salvador Ysart. Dia. 3.1", Height 1.8".
$400/500. *Author's Collection.***

Salvador Ysart only very rarely signed his paperweights with his
Y initial cane. This example is as good as his signed paperweights but, for whatever reason, does not warrant his
signature cane. These two weights demonstrate that Salvador
could make paperweights that were nearly as good as those of
his eldest son Paul, who had gone on to specialize in paperweight making, while his father's career remained firmly in art
glass. This weight has four rows of neatly placed canes set
around an open central cane. The canes sit on a turquoise
ground. Any paperweight that can be identified reliably as from
Salvador can be classed as a good find, as he made only a few
of this quality. A signature cane in the paperweight adds
another $400 to its value.

Opposite page, top right:
Four Row Concentric, Salvador Ysart. Dia. 3.1", Height 1.8". $400/500. *Courtesy of Terry and Hilary Johnson.*

This weight and the two previous paperweights attributed to Salvador Ysart, are almost identical and I would consider this weight to be as good as the signed pieces but unfortunately this piece is not signed. The off-white cane coloring with the light brown and pale blue is most attractive, with the cane rows neatly compacted together with no slippage, making this one of Salvador's best examples.

United Kingdom Paperweight, Vasart. Dia 2.9", Height 1.9". $200/250. *Courtesy of Mr. and Mrs. Richard Giles.*

An unusual and possibly unique weight, probably made as a frigger. Attributed to the Vasart Glassworks because of the similarities in base finish and coloring to known pieces. The base is slightly concave with the pontil untidily removed by grinding.

Butterfly Paperweight, Salvador Ysart. Dia. 3", Height 2". $800/1200. *Courtesy of Terry and Hilary Johnson.*

This is a very rare and beautiful butterfly, attributed to Salvador by the construction of the canes, fluorescence, and colored ground. The butterfly is hovering over the green ground which has two rows of complex but poorly made canes, but this does not detract from the lovely insect that has its wings made from flattened canes.

Inkwell, Vasart. Dia. 3.8", Height 4.1". $800/1200. *Author's Collection.*

This inkwell has better quality canes than the previous examples, being much sharper, brighter and complex.

Bird Paperweight, Salvador Ysart. Dia. 3", Height 2". $1000/1200. *Courtesy of Mr. and Mrs. Richard Giles.*

A rare and beautiful bird weight from Salvador Ysart or possibly an early attempt by Salvador's talented son Paul. The stylistic bird flies over a ground of turquoise blue on wings of flattened canes, whose tail feathers conceal a hint of red, white and yellow. A treasured addition to any collection.

Inkwell, Vasart. Dia. 3.8", Height 4.1". $600/800. *Author's Collection.*

Many inkwells were produced by Vasart, in many different pastel and pleasantly muted colors. Whichever colored ground was chosen, the color theme was followed through to the stopper. In this inkwell a pale olive green ground was used to decorate the neck of the bottle with a swirling pattern that can be found in all the inkwells produced by Vasart. The main colors used being, red, orange, blue and various shades of green. Many types of simple and complex canes can be found within the body of the inkwell with the stopper always matching the base. However, beware, this inkwell has a modern successor. Inkwells, with this swirling design in the neck are now being produced that almost replicate these early Vasart pieces. They originate in Scotland and are filled with bright Vasart type canes, with an occasional genuine cane included and can easily trap the unwary collector into thinking they have just bought an original Vasart at a bargain price. The price of these new pieces are around $100/150 and are not sold with any distinguishing marks or maker's label and no claims of attribution are made. When the seller, who is usually an antiques fair dealer, is pressed to disclose where he acquired the piece, the answer is usually "a house clearance in Scotland." The one that the author acquired was from an antique dealer at the Newark Antique Fair, England. Although I bought the only one available at the time, at the following fair three months later, this dealer in antiquities had acquired another one, identical to the piece I had bought earlier. As can be seen in the chapter on "Fakes," the piece deserves recognition in its own right as a modern copy and should be signed to identify its maker.

Inkwell, Vasart. Dia. 3.8", Height 2.75". $350/450. *Author's Collection.*

This Vasart piece has had serious damage to the quite fragile neck, which has been removed to add a brass top and lid. Although not as the maker designed, it is a good repair and an attractive feature.

Inkwell, Vasart. Dia. 3.9", Height 4". $600/800. *Courtesy of Margaret Preston.*

Orange and white candy striped spiral canes are used to separate the bright orange and pale blue, simply made canes that are set on a pale blue ground. The set-up of canes is picked up with a gather of glass during construction which has left a distinct ridge mark where the two halves are joined and can be found on many of these inkwells. The base has the pontil removed by light grinding.

Inkwell, Vasart. Dia. 3.9", Height 4.3". $700/900. *Courtesy of Margaret Preston.*

Orange was a favorite color of Vasart and can be found in slightly different shades in most of their work. This predominantly orange inkwell is also the most commonly found color in this inkwell range. The cane pattern, is followed through to the stopper which also has the slightly colored swirl pattern to match the neck of the inkwell body. These Vasart inkwells are becoming much harder to find and have risen quite significantly in price over the last few years as Salvador's work has become more recognizable and collectible.

Inkwell, Vasart. Dia. 3.9", Height 4.2". $600/800. *Courtesy of Margaret Preston.*

The central part of the body in this inkwell has a spattered ground of colored glass chippings with dark and light blue simple canes in the stopper and bulbous main body. Unusually, the neck and stopper do not have the swirl design found in most Vasart pieces, which helps with identification, but the canes in this inkwell are definitely by Vasart.

Inkwell, Salvador Ysart. Dia. 3.9", Height 4.25". $1200/ 1400. *Courtesy of Anne Metcalfe, Sweetbriar Gallery, Helsby, England.*

This is a very precisely made inkwell, which when shown to Paul Ysart, was identified as being made by his father Salvador, when he worked at Vasart. The canes are sharp and well colored and the base and stopper match. This type of Vasart inkwell could be bought for around $300 only two or three years ago, but now are in great demand with nice examples selling at auction for $1100 or more.

Concentric Paperweight, Vasart. Dia. 3", Height 1.9". $400/500. *Courtesy of Terry and Hilary Johnson.*

A simple neatly arranged concentric with an orange and blue row of canes that can be seen in a previous inkwell. A feature of many Vasart pieces is a slight blurring of the canes, as though slightly out of focus, and although not of the highest standard when compared to modern or Paul Ysart paperweights, they are still highly collectible for their rarity and historical significance.

**Concentric with Spiral Twist's, Vasart. Dia.2.9",
Height 1.9". $80/100.** *Courtesy of Terry and
Hilary Johnson.*

**Concentric Paperweight, Vasart. Dia. 3.1", Height
1.9". $100/200.** *Courtesy of Terry and Hilary Johnson.*

Bright primary colors make this weight stand out. Like
an artist's palette, the simple cog canes are set neatly
around a single, central complex cane in red, white and
black.

This paperweight shows the canes separated by
twists of spiral cane, which is a design that was
much favored by the workforce at Strathearn
during Stuart Drysdale's time in charge. After
Teacher's bought out Vasart, Stuart was brought in
as general manager and immediately set about
improving the quality of the gift weights.

**Closepacked Paperweight, Vasart. Dia. 3", Height
1.9". $100/150.** *Courtesy of Terry and Hilary
Johnson.*

A good selection of canes, but nothing of any quality
and not as well made as Salvador's. These paperweights were made as gifts, which sold for a few
dollars at the time, and were not for the collector
market of the day. They could have been made by
anyone on the workforce.

Concentric, Vasart. Dia. 3", Height 1.9". $120/150.
Courtesy of Terry and Hilary Johnson.

A varied selection of softly colored canes in the
Strathearn style. It is almost impossible to tell late
Vasart and early Strathearn paperweights apart, but
after Stuart Drysdale took charge the coloring became
much stronger with more variety and sharper defini-
tion to the canes. The spiral spoke pattern shown in
this weight was used right up to the glasswork's
closing. Before the closure most of the skilled paperweight workforce had already departed with Drysdale,
to start up Perthshire Paperweights.

Closepacked, Vasart. Dia. 3", Height 2". $200/300.
Courtesy of Margaret Preston.

This is a good closepack and has a butterfly cane within the mixed simple and complex canes that is associated with Salvador Ysart. The canes are tightly packed together, which makes the paperweight more valuable, especially if it was made by Salvador. The butterfly cane could possibly be a recognition cane by Salvador or his son Vincent as it rarely appears in Vasart weights and may be a way they identified individual pieces made by them.

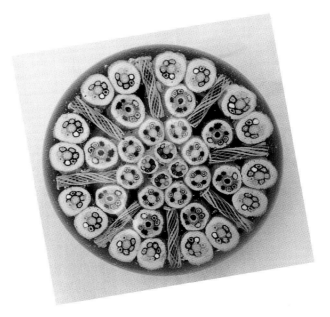

Concentric Millefiori, Vasart. Dia. 2.9", Height 2". $150/200.
Courtesy of Mr. and Mrs. Richard Giles.

Complex canes separated by spiral twists of latticinio rod make this a nice piece from Vasart. The canes are tidily placed with the rows of complex canes being of an equal matching size. Bearing a strong resemblance to Strathearn paperweights, this must have been produced around the time Vasart was bought out by William Teacher Ltd., and renamed Strathearn Glass.

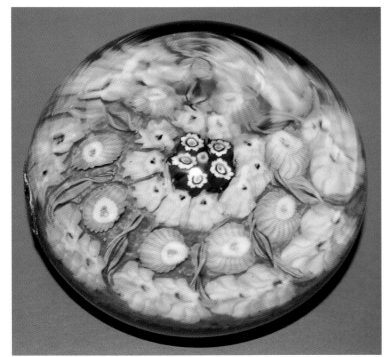

Spaced Paneled Paperweight, Vasart. Dia. 3", Height 2". $150/200.
Courtesy of Margaret Preston.

This Vasart piece was made just before Teacher's took over the company and renamed it Strathearn. As a transitional piece it could pass easily for a Strathearn if it wasn't for the label stuck to the side.

Side View of Vasart Paperweight.

Vasart rarely signed paperweights, relying on this silver and black stick-on label. Paperweights were not aimed at the high class collector market, but the cheaper gifts trade.

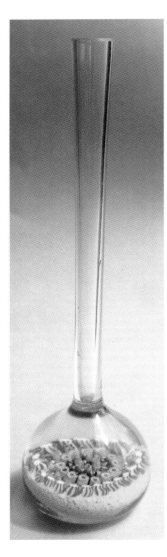

Single Rose Holder, Vasart. Height 7.5", Dia. 2.25". $30/40, *Author's Collection.*

Vasart made many varied pieces towards the end of their existence, including ashtrays, gear stick knobs and many pieces of bar equipment and door handles. When Strathearn took over the company, under Stuart Drysdale, most of these gift items were gradually discarded to concentrate on improving the quality of its paperweight production. The canes in this item are all set rather untidily, with the central feature canes merging together to form an unrecognizable dark blob.

Three Row Concentric Paperweight, Vasart. Dia. 3.1", Height 2.1". $250/350. *Author's Collection.*

This is a strange weight with unusual terra-cotta colored complex canes. The glass also has a smoky, dark tinge to it, very similar to some of the early Paul Ysart pieces and just may have been made by Paul. The outside row of white canes has a small air bubble between each cane in the same manner as Paul used to great effect in his basket weights made during his Harland years. If this piece was not made by Paul, then it is most likely by Salvador; made during the early 1930s.

Concentric with Spiral Twists, Vasart. $500/600. Dia. 3.5", Height 2.25". *Courtesy of Terry and Hilary Johnson.*

Lengths of spiral cable are twisted and pulled around the central motif of a solid yellow cog cane within a small garland of blue and white and white flower-like canes with a yellow center. Set in and above a colorful spattered ground of glass chippings, the lengths of cables are anchored to a large bubble at the front of the weight; an unusual design with a European look about it that may show the influence of Frank Eisner on the Ysarts. Frank Eisner was a glassblower at the Moncrieff Glassworks in the 1920s and 30s who originated from Europe.

Carousel Concentric Magnum Paperweight. Dia. 3.75", Height 2.7". $600/700. *Courtesy of Roy and Pam Brown.*

The spiral twists used in this weight can be found in other weights from Vasart, and as ribbon ties in Paul Ysart's flower paperweights. This weight has all the hallmarks of a Salvador-made paperweight, probably made in the 1930s when he was working alongside his talented son Paul. A sharing of millefiori canes between father and son would have been a common practice, in such a close working environment as prevailed at the Moncrieff glassworks. Although it was Paul who went on to specialize in paperweights, it would be reasonable to assume that his father, Salvador, would have been aware of Paul's activities and tried the different techniques himself, as presumably Paul's brothers did. It is usually assumed that paperweights were the domain of Salvador and Paul, but Vincent and Antoine must surely have tried their hand as well. Indeed it may be that the Y cane found in the better quality paperweights from this period were in fact made by Vincent and signed with a V. In certain weights the stem of the Y cane is quite short and could be easily mistaken for a V.

Signed Concentric Paperweight, Vasart. Dia. 3.2", Height 1.9". $800/1000. *Courtesy of Roy and Pam Brown.*

This superb paperweight, from either Salvador or Vincent, demonstrates how ambiguous this signature cane can be, as, in this example, the cane in the second row from the edge looks more like a V than a Y. When I asked non-paperweight friends to tell me their first impression of the signature cane, the answer for this weight is always a V, but in other signed weights with this signature cane, the answer can vary either way. I am sure there must be someone out there, who worked with the Ysarts, who can tell us the answer.

Concentric, Vasart. Dia. 3.1", Height 2". $400/600. *Author's Collection.*

A five-row concentric with several rows made from very complex canes in approximately 30 varieties, including a cane with a white butterfly on a red ground in the third row from the edge. The complex cane in the outer edge is a common cane that is often seen in Strathearn paperweights.

Fountain and Latticinio Basket Paperweight, Salvador Ysart. Dia. 3.9", Height 3.5". $1000/1500. *Courtesy of Terry and Hilary Johnson.*

This very rare and unusual piece, of magnum proportions, was probably made in the 1930s by Salvador Ysart. Another similar paperweight with a latticinio basket has recently been found with a butterfly hovering over the basket. The butterfly in that weight has all the characteristics of Salvador's style, and is described in detail by John Simmonds in the 1998 PCA Annual Bulletin. The glass dome on this fountain paperweight has a slightly dark tinge, which is similar to early Ysart pieces made around the 1930s. The colored spirals of the fountains are made in a similar way to early Ysart ribbons and could be that this weight was made by Paul Ysart or any one of the Ysart family. The pontil has been left unground in the way Paul Ysart left the majority of his bases. A large bubble decorates the center of the fountain.

Top View of Salvador Ysart Fountain Paperweight.

Upright Flower Paperweight, Ysart. Dia. 1.7", Height 3.25". $400/ 500. *Courtesy of Roy and Pam Brown.*

An unusual tall paperweight that may have been made by Paul Ysart because of the meticulous finish to the piece but could be more consistent with a Salvador attribution, and made at Moncrieff's in the late 1930s or 40s. Salvador may have experimented with three-dimensional flowers after seeing another glassmaker named Frank Eisner make similar flowers as an experiment. The Ysarts never allowed anyone other than themselves to develop the art glass and paperweight side of the business and were a dominant force at the factory. One concession was made to Frank Eisner, who was allowed to make simple paperweights of one type of flower only, in his spare time.

Four Flower Paperweight, Frank Eisner. Dia. 3.4", Height 2.6". $300/400. *Courtesy of Terry and Hilary Johnson.*

Most people would immediately recognize the following four paperweights as early 20th century Bohemian or Eastern European, but in fact these paperweights were made by Frank Eisner at the Moncrieff glassworks in the 1930s. Coming from a European heritage, Frank Eisner worked alongside the Ysart family and developed this flower type of paperweight in his spare time. Little is known about Eisner except that the four paperweights shown here came directly from him in the early 1990s via a Perth dealer who knew him and his family. The paperweights all fluoresce in exactly the same way as early Ysart paperweights made around 1930–1940 at Moncrieff's, and were made from the same batch of glass as that used by the Ysarts.

Four Flower Paperweight, Frank Eisner. Dia. 3.4", Height 2.6". $300/400. *Courtesy of Terry and Hilary Johnson.*

Three Flower Paperweight, Frank Eisner. Dia. 3.4", Height 2.6". $300/400. *Courtesy of Terry and Hilary Johnson.*

The identification of most of the Vasart pieces has been confirmed by the use of an ultraviolet light. Using a high quality light, Vasart paperweights and related objects fluoresce gray in the short wave, and green in the long wave. Both short and long wave lights should be used in identification as Strathearn products fluoresce blue in the short wave and green in the long wave.

Four Flower Paperweight, Frank Eisner. Dia. 3.4", Height 2.6". $300/400 *Courtesy of Terry and Hilary Johnson.*

CHAPTER 5

STRATHEARN LTD, 1965-1980

Crieff, Scotland

Strathearn Glass Ltd came into existence in January 1965 and was a custom built factory owned by William Teacher & Sons. The management and staff were all ex-workers of Vasart Glass Ltd. Vasart was unable to meet demand for orders placed by Teacher's for a novelty ashtray made from a collapsed whisky bottle and used for advertising purposes, so Teacher's bought the company and moved the business from Perth to Crieff just a few miles away. This new glass house began producing many of the lines made by Vasart and increased production of the ashtrays to 4,000 per month. The management team comprised of Stuart Drysdale as general manager and Vincent Ysart as works manager. Angus Sillars was the design director and supervised the designs of paperweights and art glass in the Vasart style.

The general paperweights made by Strathearn in this new factory showed a marked improvement over the general weights produced by Vasart. This improvement in quality was insisted on by the management and new owners, as they were very conscious of the tourist potential of a shop on the premises. The glass vases and bowls made at Strathearn were marked on the base by an impressed leaping salmon motif over the pontil mark. Paperweights were not permanently marked in any way in the beginning, but eventually an "S" cane and a black-and-silver paper label were used. The weights showed very little variation in style, usually concentric millefiori canes separated by radiating filigree canes, but were executed carefully and in many color variations. A few lampworked and spaced millefiori on lace paperweights were

made, and occasionally these were signed with an S cane with the date. Among other weights that can be found with a signature cane are the small limited edition weights which comprised double overlays and crown weights. The range of weights produced in unlimited editions were concentric, close-packed and spaced millefiori, and could be found in a variety of sizes from miniature to magnum. Most were rather poor copies in the style of antique French paperweights, but towards the end of production in the late 1970s the quality of canes and setting had greatly improved with many pieces being of collector quality, even though they were destined for the cheaper gift outlets.

Vincent Ysart left the company in 1966 to follow a career elsewhere outside of the glass industry, and the general manager left in 1968 after a dispute with the owners over the direction the company was taking. Stuart Drysdale was in favor of following in the footsteps of the old French masters of paperweight making after having read an article on antique paperweights in *Woman's Day* magazine. Drysdale was very interested in trying to recapture some of the lost techniques of the old French Glass houses, but Strathearn's owners wanted volume production to cater to the gifts trade, which could only be met by producing abstract weights.

Strathearn was a profitable company during its relatively short life as a paperweight maker, but with the decline in the popularity of the collapsed ashtray, Teacher's eventually sold the business in 1980 to the Stourbridge firm of Stuart Crystal, who promptly closed paperweight production to concentrate on making blanks to be shipped to the parent company in Stourbridge, where they were cut and engraved.

The former Strathearn Glassworks, Crieff, Scotland. (Now owned by Stuart Crystal.)

This is the building that William Teacher & Son built to house the glassmakers from Vasart when production outgrew their previous small glassworks in Perth. Most of the Vasart workers moved the few miles from Perth to Crieff to continue in their craft. At present, glassmaking has ceased and it is now a large retail showroom for Stuart Crystal.

Stuart Crystal still owns the premises in Crieff but no longer makes glass, although the factory is still popular with tourists, who can watch demonstrations of engraving and cutting and visit a well stocked gift and coffee shop. The workshop area also undertakes small repairs to chipped and damaged glass.

Paperweight, Strathearn. Dia. 3", Height 2". $75/100. *Courtesy of Terry and Hilary Johnson.*

This early Strathearn weight shows canes in the center which can be found in Vasart paperweights, and shows that millefiori canes outlive the life of the glassworks that made them. This piece has very little quality about it, but on the outside row is an unusual cane that could be elements of a date cane. As Strathearn had ceased production of paperweights in 1980, it cannot be a date cane for 1988. Strathearn occasionally dated weights with just two numerals. This same cane has been found in a selection of canes held by the now closed Royal Brierley Crystal Museum, Stourbridge, England. The museum was given the canes, which were thought to have been made by themselves, but in fact, the canes had been left by a group of trainee glassworkers from Strathearn on a training scheme. The trainees had brought the canes with them from Scotland. Royal Brierley Crystal and Teacher's Whiskey Ltd., who owned Strathearn, had close business links, and an interchange of skills and workers was not an uncommon practice.

Paneled Paperweight, Strathearn. Dia. 3", Height 2". $100/150. *Courtesy of Terry and Hilary Johnson.*

The colors of Strathearn weights are much stronger than Vasart, and the canes have sharper detail and are relatively easy to identify but, unfortunately, not many were signed or dated, with the exception of later lampworked pieces. This type of paneled millefiori paperweight has been the mainstay of many British collections. These relatively cheap paperweights, readily found at most antique markets and fairs, can be an attractive and collectible area for a collector new to paperweights, and with Strathearn prices rising, as these weights are collected and put away, they could prove to be a valuable asset in the near future.

Paneled Paperweight, Strathearn. Dia. 3", Height 2". $100/150. *Courtesy of Terry and Hilary Johnson.*

The distinguishing feature in this Strathearn weight is the separating latticinio rods, in this case the rods have been straight pulled without any twist being imparted to the rod. The quality of these weights are certainly an improvement on their earlier counterparts from Vasart but, because of the large number made at Strathearn, their value is less than the rarer Vasart paperweights.

**Signed and Dated Paneled Paperweight, Strathearn. Dia. 3",
Height 2". $150/250.** *Courtesy of Terry and Hilary Johnson.*

A rare signed and dated Strathearn paneled weight. The date cane
on the outside is only two numerals and the center cane has a red S
on a white ground, also to be found in blue on other pieces. There
is enough variety in color and design of these paneled weights to
make an interesting collection.

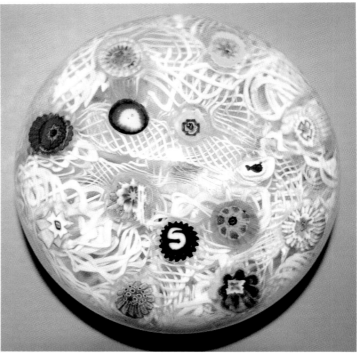

Spaced Concentric on Lace, Strathearn. 1969. $450/600.
Courtesy of Anne Anderson.

This is an extremely good paperweight from Strathearn, with plenty
of variety in the canes and with a silhouette of a black cat, a large
signature cane, and is also dated on the base with a 69 cane. This
weight shows a great improvement over the previous example and
is a desirable collector piece.

**Paneled Paperweight with Flower Canes, Strathearn. Dia. 3.1",
Height 2.25". $100/180.** *Author's Collection.*

This pretty weight would command a slightly higher than average
price among collectors because the primrose colored canes around
the central motif have an interpretation of a white flower with a
blue center within the cane. This is the only one I have seen with
this feature and is a treasured piece. The set-up rests on a pink
ground; colored grounds are a feature of nearly all weights from
Strathearn.

**Spaced Paperweight on Latticinio, Strathearn. $100/150.
Dia. 2.9 ", Height 1.9".** *Courtesy of Terry and Hilary
Johnson.*

The French 19th century glassworks of Clichy perfected this
style of spaced canes on latticinio or muslin as its sometimes
called. The antique version would sell for around $2000, and
although this Strathearn piece is rare in comparison to the
paneled type, it still does not have the quality of canes, or
setting, as its French, antique equivalent but is still a valued
addition to a new collection.

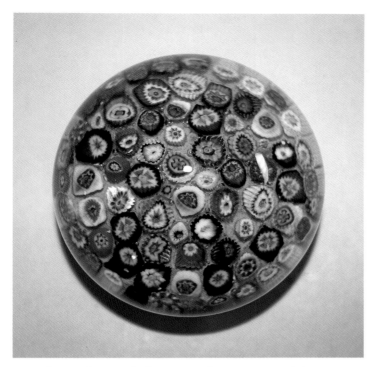

A three-dimensional flower that is dated 73 and signed S. This flower and petals can be found in other colors and usually "growing" over a colored ground but sometimes found over latticinio spirals.

Strathearn Close Packed Paperweight. Dia. 2.9", Height 2.25". $100/150. *Author's Collection.*

Plenty of cane variety but most are slightly misshapen and of odd sizes. Close packs were not made in the same quantities as paneled weights but would be priced a little less because of a general untidiness.

Lampworked Primroses, Strathearn. Dia. 3", Height 2.25". $150/250. *Courtesy of Terry and Hilary Johnson.*

An early and creditable attempt with the lampworking torch from an unknown Strathearn glassmaker. The flowers are well constructed but the buds do not connect to the main stem. This is a rare paperweight and very collectible as very few lampworked pieces were made.

Close Pack with Facets, Strathearn. Dia.3", Height 1.75". $150/250. *Author's Collection.*

This is a better attempt at a close pack with care going into the cane sizing and positioning. A good selection of complex canes set on a turquoise ground. Six and one faceting with a flat, ground base makes this one of the better pieces from Strathearn, and of collector quality.

**Crown Paperweight, Strathearn. Dia. 2.75", Height 2".
$150/250. *Courtesy of Terry and Hilary Johnson.***

An unusual and rare Crown weight from Strathearn with
the orange colored ribs showing through a powdered glass.

**Commemorative Paperweight, Strathearn. $100/150. Dia 3",
Height 2.5". *Courtesy of Terry and Hilary Johnson.***

During Strathearn's fifteen-year existence they were very commercial minded and took on many commissions from companies for
giftware and paperweights. This paperweight example was produced in 1977 for Queen Elizabeth's Jubilee year. A simple garland
of red and white canes around an engraved ER makes a stylish
paperweight, identified with a Strathearn sticker on the base.

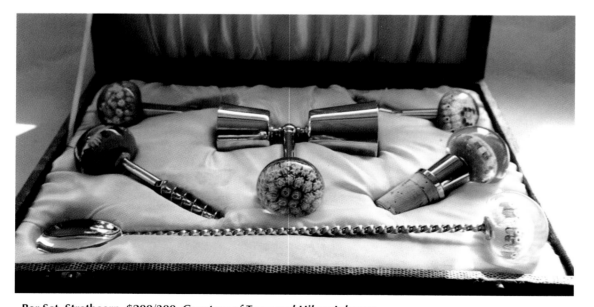

Bar Set, Strathearn. $200/300. *Courtesy of Terry and Hilary Johnson.*

This presentation set of spirit measures, swizzle sticks, corkscrew and bottle stoppers would be considered a
must for every cocktail bar in the early 1970s, and quite a few were sold, but it is extremely rare to find a
set that is complete. Many pieces turn up in antiques fairs but usually only single items. So it is nice to see a
complete set in the original box.

CHAPTER 6

Perthshire Paperweights Ltd, Founded 1968

Crieff, Scotland

In 1967 Stuart Drysdale was the manager of Strathearn Glass Ltd. Based in Crieff, the company was involved in many aspects of glass production including paperweights. These paperweights had been gradually improving in variety and quality since Drysdale became manager. Although he had no glassmaking skills to contribute, he was an astute business man with an artistic flair who had begun his career as a country lawyer. During his two years at Strathearn, and a further five years at the same glassworks under their previous name, Vasart, the workforce had steadily improved on the paperweights the company had been making and were now respected by the collecting public. The owners of the company at this time were William Teacher's Ltd, a giant whisky distillery, who had little interest in developing paperweights into a major part of the Strathearn business.

Stuart Drysdale was a man of vision, and after being shown an article in the magazine *Woman's Day* on antique French paperweights, he had visualized his future career as a quality paperweight producer. He knew that the workforce he had under him at Strathearn had all the necessary skills to reproduce these complicated objects of beauty. So he gave the company due notice and by February 1968 had found premises at an old Catholic school in Crieff and fitted it out. With the best of the skilled paperweight makers on the Strathearn workforce leaving the company to join Drysdale in his new venture, Perthshire Paperweights began in business.

The workers who had joined the firm at this time included Peter McDougal, Jack Allen, Roy McDonald, John Deacons and Anton Moravic. Jack Allen was the Master Gaffer on the team, and was instrumental in passing on his expertise to the younger men. The old school premises were adequate for the fledgling business in the beginning, but very shortly the paperweights that were being produced were in such demand, being of such good quality in design and artistry, that they realized they needed bigger quarters to meet this increasing demand. After only two years in business they moved to a much larger custom-built glassworks in Crieff, here they could grow into and further their quest for better and even more beautiful paperweights.

Today the company is at the forefront of the paperweight market in design, technology and innovative products. Still under the guidance of the Drysdale family, the company produces in excess of 20,000 paperweights every year. Most will be destined for the top end of the gift market; with just a few made for the serious and discerning paperweight collectors. These collector pieces are the result of the amazing skills of a dedicated workforce, who with the guidance of Neil Drysdale and Peter McDougal, are pushing out the boundaries in this wonderful art form. From the company's formation in 1968 most weights made were unsigned with the exception of the limited editions made for the collector market. However, from 1974 on, all weights made by Perthshire Paperweights were signed with a P cane somewhere in the weight. Most paperweights are destined for a buoyant home market, but approximately 30 percent are exported to the USA and many other countries, with new markets opening in the Far East and Japan. These markets are continually fed with new designs every year.

The company aims to produce seventeen to twenty new designs annually, with limited editions of only two or three hundred. The first limited edition in 1969 was a crown weight made by Jack Allen and designed by Alan Tilman, limited to 350 pieces and sold for $60. As an indication of investment value, several of these crown weights have recently been sold through auction houses realizing $900. Several special pieces are made on commission with editions as small as five, but with a price of around $1500. There are many weights that are overlayed and faceted with superb inclusions of flowers and millefiori canes that can still be bought for around $600 to $800 from dealers, with some early pieces from the 1970s in great demand from collectors.

The Perthshire Paperweight Company lays claim to a first in paperweight design and innovation, they have produced a triple encased, triple overlay in a limited edition of five. This technique of encasing paperweights is an extremely difficult operation which had been tried by the French makers and by Bacchus of England in the 1850s. The process entails the slow cooling of a piece which can then be engraved or faceted, and then returned to the annealing ovens and furnace to be brought back up to a sufficient temperature to enable another gather of glass to be added. This process is repeated three times, overlaying the weight with different colors. Surely this must be the pinnacle of paperweight making. This company continues to astound the collector with its newest pieces, and one can only wonder what the future holds in design innovation.

A Selection of Early Canes signed with a letter P and the date.

World's First Triple Encased, Triple Overlay Paperweight. *Courtesy of Perthshire Paperweights.*

A wonderful, innovative creation from the master craftsmen of Perthshire Paperweights. The skills and technical expertise of many people have gone into this limited edition of five special weights. Many weights would have been lost to the scrap bin before this type of paperweight could be perfected. The many technical dangers encountered in the construction of the individual layers due to the glass contracting unevenly in the heating and cooling process, have deterred many glass houses from even trying to make this type of weight as uneconomical and time consuming, This encasement process has been demonstrated only sparingly since the 19th century.

Spaced Millefiori on Lace, 1969. $250/350 *Courtesy of Anne Anderson.*

A very early piece that is dated on the base 1969, and already shows a marked improvement from the Strathearn weights. The range of cane designs have now become much sharper and complex with stronger color.

1969 Crown Paperweight. $700/900. *Courtesy of Perthshire Paperweights.*

Perthshire Paperweights started producing weights in 1968, but this special piece is the first paperweight to be issued by the company in a limited edition. The edition size was 350 and quickly sold out. Possibly because it was the first collector's crown weight of real quality at a time when collectors were aware that, to acquire a quality crown weight would have meant buying at auction a Saint Louis or similar antique, for several thousand dollars. The weight was made by Jack Allen and designed by Alan Tilman and was sold for $60.These crown weights appear quite regularly at auction in the USA and through dealers in the UK. They are eagerly bought by collectors for quite considerable sums anxious to acquire these special pieces.

First Fruit Paperweight from Early 1970s. $400/600. *Courtesy of Perthshire Paperweights.*

Many of the early weights made by Perthshire are influenced by the French Classic weights of the 19th century. This design was very popular with the Saint Louis Glassworks, France, and the Perthshire men were quick to perfect the design. Stuart Drysdale had seen an article on French weights made around 1850 and encouraged his workforce to use the antique weights as a guide, whilst trying to recreate and improve on these classic pieces. This weight has two pears, an orange and three cherries resting on a bed of leaves, with a lacy bed of latticinio around the base. Many other types of fruit were also used to great effect including oranges, grapes and vegetables.

Faceted Square-Cut Dahlia Paperweight. $400/600. *Courtesy of Perthshire Paperweights.*

An early lampworked design of a dahlia made in 1972. The multi-layers of pink petals are centered on a complex millefiori cane. The lampwork skills needed to make the petals in this lifelike representation are quite remarkable. A uniformity of petal size is needed to make this piece realistic, which has been achieved to a very high standard.

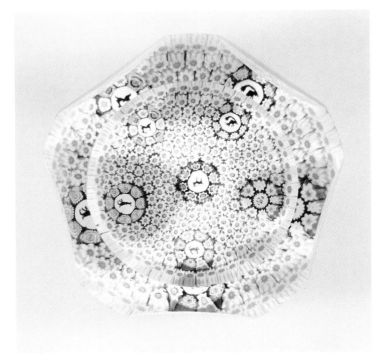

Faceted Carpet Ground with Silhouette Canes. $350/500. *Courtesy of Perthshire Paperweights.*

This weight has several copies of the Gridel silhouette canes used so successfully in antique Baccarat weights c.1850. Emil Gridel was an employee at Baccarat, whose small son had drawn pictures of animals which became the inspiration for Emil to design silhouette canes to be inserted into paperweights. Among the silhouettes used in this weight are a dog, squirrel, deer, and goat. The weight is signed with a P and 1973 date cane.

Pansy Paperweight. $300/400. *Courtesy of Perthshire Paperweights.*

Made in 1971, this pansy design was a favorite of the Victorian makers who made it in many colors and sizes. Here it is shown to great effect on a bed of latticinio spiral canes and then garlanded with complex blue and pink canes. A very pretty weight of great charm that was full of symbolism for the French people in the 19th century. A gift of a pansy symbolized tender thoughts and was also discreetly worn as an emblem of support for the deposed Napoleon Bonaparte.

Flash Overlay. 1971. *Courtesy of Perthshire Paperweights.*

This is the first overlay the company tried in 1970 and was a complete success, made and signed by Jack Allen and Anton Moravic The overlay paperweight is now a company standard, which they have used innovatively with great effect. The five complex millefiori canes are centered on a large central complex cane and then lightly overlayed in red glass. Five side facets with smaller round printies and a large top window allows the pattern to be viewed within.

Flash Overlay before and after cutting. *Courtesy of Perthshire Paperweights.*

A posy of seven flowers tied with a yellow ribbon is enclosed within this lightly overlayed weight. The use of a thin outer flash of color can greatly enhance the attractiveness of a weight.Cutting through the overlay in a diamond pattern adds value and interest to these lovely weights.

Overlayed Butterfly Paperweight. $400/600. *Courtesy of Perthshire Paperweights.*

A superb interpretation of a butterfly on a clover flower set inside this deep red and white double overlay. A large viewing window has been cut on the top with large and small side printies to show off the overlay to its best advantage.

Faceted Mushroom Paperweight. $250/350. *Courtesy of Perthshire Paperweights.*

Enhanced by the all-over faceting, this millefiori mushroom has a wide variety of complex cogs and star canes in many colors to keep the viewer interested. An added attraction is the use of two different canes around the outer edge of the mushroom. By interspacing yellow and green canes, when the mushroom is pulled down to the base to make the stalk, it creates a very attractive pattern.

Cambridge Paperweight Circle Commission. *Courtesy Perthshire Paperweights.*

Many commissions are undertaken by Perthshire as can be seen with this example. In this case the flower design was submitted by members of this collectors club, based in Cambridge, England, for the company to produce as a commemorative piece for club members only.

Christmas Paperweights. *Courtesy of Perthshire Paperweights.*

A representative collection of Christmas weights made during the 1980s and 1990s. These weights have been made in limited editions of several hundred since the company was formed. One year was omitted in 1973. These weights are eagerly collected by Perthshire enthusiasts worldwide.

Newel Post. *Courtesy of Perthshire Paperweights.*

A large newel post of magnum proportions demonstrates the worker's skills and shows that anything made in the past can now be recreated by the Perthshire workforce. The Newel post was a popular item made by all the antiques makers in the 1850s and would be found at the bottom of the grand staircase in many wealthy households. This copy shows as many variations of millefiori canes as the original. This superbly crafted piece is indeed a tribute to the Perthshire workforce who made it.

Encased Double Overlay with Butterflies. *Courtesy of Perthshire Paperweights.*

Made in an edition of only five pieces, this superb paperweight was made as a special order for a customer and was not for resale. The weight shows two pretty butterflies hovering over clover type flowers within a double overlay that has been deeply cut and patterned. After being cut and patterned, the weight was returned to the annealing oven to be reheated and then encased in another gather of glass.

Crown and Basket Paperweight. $600/700. *Courtesy of Perthshire Paperweights.*

Made in 1981, this is a rare test piece of an extremely fine quality. A perfectly made latticinio basket is supporting a six-petal flower and leaves, which is then gently lowered onto a very attractive green and blue crown weight. Beautifully centered, to make this piece quite perfect and a joy to admire and hold.

One-Off Test Piece. *Courtesy of Perthshire Paperweights.*

A spray of flowers sits on a Ruby flashed base, multi-faceting enhances the internal design.

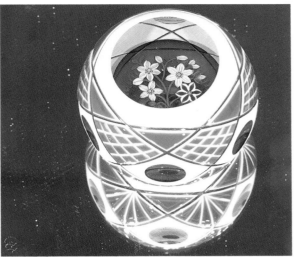

One-Off Test Piece. *Courtesy of Perthshire Paperweights.*

A spray of different colored flowers can be found inside this test piece, with the top coat of green glass ground away to expose the white glass beneath. Cut into a lattice work pattern with six side windows and a large top window to view the inside, the pattern adds interest and formality to the whole weight.

One-Off Test Piece. *Courtesy of Perthshire Paperweights.*

Flowers with buds and berries and a difficult type of double overlay. The outer layer of green glass has been ground away to leave an all-white panel. This cutting is extremely skilled; only a small slip would ruin the pattern. The cutter of this weight showed great dexterity on the cutting wheel.

One-Off Test Piece. *Courtesy of Perthshire Paperweights.*

A dark blue double overlay precisely ground with a star cut base that frames the posy of flowers perfectly. Viewed from below, the weight is almost as attractive as seen from above. The color contrast of dark blue and white is the most striking of combinations in a double overlay and highly valued in collecting circles.

One-Off Test Piece. *Courtesy of Perthshire Paperweights.*

Fancy cutting on the base adds interest to this piece. The dark blue and white double overlay has been cut in a lattice pattern with the underlying white glass removed from the central area to frame a variety of colored flowers within. A superb and precise weight, made with the utmost care and thought.

One-Off Test Piece. *Courtesy of Perthshire Paperweights.*

A crystal clear paperweight which has a spray of flowers seemingly resting against a trellis framework, formed by deep cutting on the base. A garland of interwoven white flowers and red berries frames the whole design. A masterpiece of design and construction.

Peter McDougal and John Parsley working together on a Collaborative Paperweight. *Courtesy of Perthshire Paperweights.*

Two supreme craftsmen at work on a piece designed and made together. Peter gets the final shape perfect before the weight is broken from the pontil and placed in the annealing oven, to slowly cool before being cut and polished. This slow cooling process can take up to 24 hours.

Collaborative Paperweight. *Courtesy of Perthshire Paperweights.*

The finished product is a stunning wild red rose with berries and deeply veined green leaves. Made in a limited edition of 12, each weight has a joint signature cane PM/JP. The weight is surrounded by a garland of blue and white complex millefiori canes and cut with six and one faceting. The spray of flowers sits on a bed of white latticinio to finish the weight off to a high standard.

Magnum Millefiori with Silhouette Canes. *Courtesy of Perthshire Paperweights.*

An amazing and unique variety of silhouette canes can be found around the center of this special weight. They include a horse and rider, fly, penguin, tree and an eagle. A large selection of complex canes are evenly spaced between lengths of short latticinio, and red and yellow twisted canes. A double tier of round facets with a large window on the top helps to make this a most impressive weight and not just because of the magnum size.

Molded Concentric Millefiori. *Author's Collection.*

Two of the standard molded weights that are the mainstay of Perthshire Paperweights. This type of weight is produced by the thousand and has been the beginning of many a collection. Amazing value for the money at around $30/40 they make ideal gifts to encourage new collectors. Although sold cheaply, they are not cheaply made. All the skills of the master paperweight makers have been used to get a paperweight of this quality to the retailers at this introductory price. Every one is signed with a P and in the center of the other one can be seen PCA. Every delegate at the 1997 Paperweight Collectors Conference in San Diego, California, was given a commemorative keepsake by Perthshire Paperweights.

Concentric Millefiori. Dia. 3". $75/100. *Author's Collection.*

Cog canes in red, pink, brown, blue and white. Simply designed canes, but when gathered together in this concentric pattern, they form a lovely pattern that has collectors worldwide seeking the many variations of this spoke type. The cane set-up rests on a pale blue ground.

Concentric Millefiori. Dia. 3".
$75/100. *Author's Collection.*

The signature cane in this weight is on a white tablet on the base dated 1977 P. A slight variation on the concentric theme but different enough to tempt a serious collector, "I haven't got that one," he exclaims, as he parts with his cash and another one is added to the collection. The set-up sits on a dark blue flashed ground.

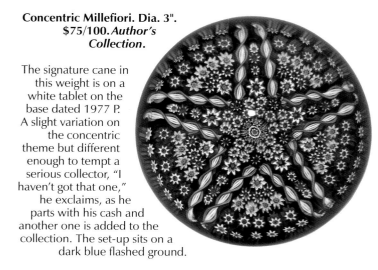

Concentric Millefiori. Dia. 2.5". Height 1.75". $50/75. *Author's Collection.*

A slightly smaller version of the last weight. This one measures 2.5 inches in diameter and is an early weight from this glass house; it is unsigned. The canes sit on a pink ground, with the base unground and slightly concave.

Patterned Millefiori. Dia. 3". Height 2". $75/100. *Author's Collection.*

An early unsigned paperweight which shows the influence of the French Clichy glassworks of the mid 19th century on Perthshire. The central pink cane looks very similar in construction to the famous Clichy pastry mold canes. A delightful weight with the cane set-up resting on a mint green ground. The base is unground but smoothed by the glassmaker to remove the pontil mark.

Patterned Millefiori. Dia. 3" Height 2.1" $75/100 *Author's Collection.*

Signed with a tiny P in the central cane, this precisely set paperweight is sectioned by colored spiral twists of cane. A garland of spiral cane and pale yellow canes holds the piece in harmony. Set on a pale blue ground of powdered glass, with the base neatly finished by grinding to a slight concavity.

Maltese Cross Dia. 2.9". Height 1.9". $200/300. *Author's Collection.*

Signed and dated 1987 this superb use of millefiori canes is a tribute to the craftsmen and designers at Perthshire Paperweights. The use of pink and blue canes are always a nice combination in a weight, and with the latticinio threads high-lighting the cross, this paperweight is on a par with the very best from Whitefriars and the antique glass factories of France.

Commemorative Paperweight in Honor of Stuart Drysdale.
Courtesy of Perthshire Paperweights.

In 1990, Stuart Drysdale, founder and supreme driving force behind Perthshire Paperweights died. His son Neil took control of the company and has continued in his father's place, striving to keep the company ahead in its quest for the ultimate in paperweight designs. This piece was made to commemorate his father's career in paperweights and was gifted to the Bergstrom Mahler Museum in the USA, to be added to their already fine and rare paperweight display. The magnum weight was created in gleaming crystal of the highest clarity with faceting all over to make the piece sparkle with light. The spray of pink and white flowers fills the inside of the weight and is tied with a spiral of twisted ribbon.

Anniversary Paperweight. *Courtesy of Perthshire Paperweights.*

In 1993, a 25th Anniversary paperweight was produced. A striking combination of millefiori canes and lampwork, with an added bonus of canes that look as though they have been sliced in half to create dahlia-type petals.

First Fish Paperweight. *Courtesy of Perthshire Paperweights.*

Long fronds of seaweed hide several colorful fish in a crystal clear glass. All over faceting makes the weight alive and vibrant. Peering into the depths, the viewer could almost expect to see the lifelike tropical fish move.

Neil Drysdale at The Artist's Fair, Wheaton Village, USA.

Perthshire Paperweights collection for 1998, proudly displayed by Neil Drysdale at The Artist's Fair in May 1998. The collection shows several "one-off" weights including Magnum and overlay paperweights. To the right of the photograph can be seen an example of Perthshire humor. Displayed on a wooden plinth are a glass hammer, screwdriver, nails and screws; an exercise by Perthshire's skilled workers to demonstrate the many uses of crystal glass around the home.

Peter McDougal. *Courtesy of Perthshire Paperweights.*

Peter McDougal has been with the company from the day it started back in 1968, he worked alongside Stuart Drysdale, designing, creating the canes and making weights of the highest caliber. Although much of his time is taken with administrative duties, he is trying to dedicate more time to creative paperweight making, a task he loves.

Chic Young. *Courtesy of Perthshire Paperweights.*

Master glassblower Chic Young, although now retired, worked for many years at Perthshire Paperweights and came to be one of the most respected and skilled of all Scottish glassworkers. Held in high esteem by his fellow workers at Perthshire Paperweights.

Setting Millefiori Canes. *Courtesy of Perthshire Paperweights.*

Millefiori canes are cut to quarter-inch lengths and then set in pattern molds before going into the glassworks to be encased in a dome of crystal. The task is slow and skilled, as all canes have to be sized to match its neighbor with each piece picked up with tweezers and placed into position. No gaps between the canes can be allowed otherwise slippage and distortion occurs.

The Final Inspection by Marrolyn Williamson. *Courtesy of Perthshire Paperweights.*

Head of the inspection and dispatch department, Marrolyn Williamson has the final say, whether a weight is be despatched to a customer or the waste bin. Strict guidelines mean no imperfect weights leave the factory.

Duncan Smith. *Courtesy of Perthshire Paperweights.*

Duncan Smith is the man responsible for the wonderful lampwork presently being made at Perthshire Paperweights. Working to a design formula but with a certain amount of artistic license, he has succeeded in creating lampwork of the highest order.

The Viewing Gallery at Perthshire Paperweights.

The viewing gallery is the most popular of the attractions at this glassworks, visitors are allowed to touch the many wonderful weights produced here, but only those embedded in the concrete on top of the wall. For the general browser this allows a close-up look at many of the company's top weights.

Lampwork Set-Ups. *Courtesy of Perthshire Paperweights.*

A selection of lampwork created by Duncan Smith, including fuschias and the Scottish thistle.

As the *pièce de résistance* from this company, Perthshire Paperweights have recently produced a one-off special commission for one of its American customers. This is one of the largest and most complicated paperweights ever made by the company, and has 35 flower heads within the multi-faceted crystal paperweight. The magnificent lampworked flowers include a yellow rose, and other flowers in red, blue, white and lilac colors, with many buds.

Magnum Bouquet, Gingham Cut Double Overlay, Encased with Another Double Overlay. Dia. 4.5". $1500/2000.
Courtesy of Terry and Hilary Johnson.

This demonstration of technical wizardry puts Perthshire Paperweights at the top of the league in paperweight terms. Not only are the rose-like flowers and buds beautifully made, but then a double overlay in red and white is applied, a difficult and laborious gingham pattern is cut in, and further encased in a gather of clear glass, which is also double overlayed and cut Gingham style. It beggars belief.

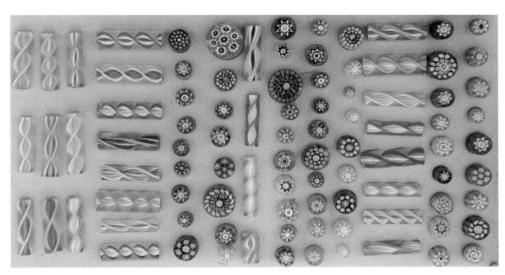

Selection of Canes. *Courtesy of Perthshire Paperweights.*

A varied and colorful selection of canes in daily use at Perthshire Paperweights. Starting with simple cog and star canes, the rods are bundled together, reheated and drawn out to make even more complex canes. There is no limit to the number of times this operation can be performed, gradually reducing the cane motif to the complexity required.

Close-Up of Canes.

Approximately 75 segments of cane are required to produce this complex green and pink cane, which is a representation of a Pom-Pom dahlia. This tiny cane measuring only half an inch in diameter can be con-joined with similar canes, heated again and drawn out to make a cane with many hundreds of segments that would need a strong loop to see the individual parts. Canes of this complexity are only used in the finest of collector pieces because of the time and expense of making such a beautiful cane.

CHAPTER 7

PAUL YSART, THE CAITHNESS YEARS, 1963 TO 1970

Caithness Glass, Wick, Scotland

In 1963, Paul Ysart was offered the position of Training and Technical Officer at the Caithness glassworks on the outskirts of Wick, a small town at the northernmost tip of Scotland. While Paul worked at Caithness, he only made paperweights in his spare time or as experimental pieces. His role was to teach new workers and apprentices the rudiments of glassmaking, but the more talented of his protégés were also taught the skills involved in paperweight making.

The seven years Paul stayed at Caithness were to become his most productive in terms of new designs and sophisticated subjects. His experimentation led him to areas of very new and detailed concepts in paperweight making. He began to make animals and birds at the lamp, where he could express his artistry and then take his creations to be embedded forever in glass. Paul enjoyed this freedom and worked after hours and weekends producing small amounts of fine weights. Some of these weights included designs and styles he had made throughout his career and included posy weights in baskets and single flowers. It would be fair to say that after thirty or so years of fine paperweight making the weights produced during his Caithness period could be regarded as among his finest works and were usually faultless. Paperweights made by Paul in this factory fluoresce blue in the short wave and green in the long wave.

Snake Paperweight, Paul Ysart. Dia. 2.5", Height 1.8". Archive Photo. $1400/1600. *Courtesy of Anne Metcalfe, Sweetbriar Gallery, Helsby, England.*

Paul Ysart produced many snake weights while working at Caithness, and in one year it was recorded that he made 150 of the same snake, but for all of this volume, very few have actually re-emerged on to the collecting market, which is why they are so sought after at auction. A few were made with less detail and would be expected to sell for $200/300 less than this example. This orange spotted reptile lies coiled on a bright green ground with scattered rocks. Signed with a PY cane.

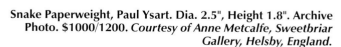

Snake Paperweight, Paul Ysart. Dia. 2.5", Height 1.8". Archive Photo. $1000/1200. *Courtesy of Anne Metcalfe, Sweetbriar Gallery, Helsby, England.*

A pink coiled snake with the spots reaching half way down its body, on a green ground with mixed mica flecks.

Snake Paperweight, Paul Ysart. Dia. 2.7", Height 2". Archive Photo. $1200/1400. *Courtesy of Anne Metcalfe. Sweetbriar Gallery, Helsby, England.*

A realistic coiled snake on a green ground in clear glass. The snake is made from tightly twisted spiral cane with black eyes and red mouth. The weight is footed and signed with a PY cane.

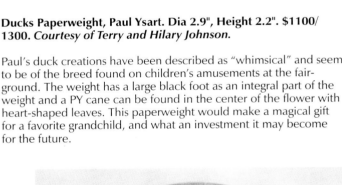

Footed Snake Paperweight, Paul Ysart. Dia. 2.9", Height 2.25. $1800/2200. *Courtesy of Terry and Hilary Johnson.*

Two coiled snakes of different varieties face each other on a pale green ground. Both snakes are superbly detailed with spots and wavy stripe from head to tail. The crystal clear glass has been formed with a black foot which gives the impression of a stand, but is part of the whole piece.

Ducks Paperweight, Paul Ysart. Dia 2.9", Height 2.2". $1100/1300. *Courtesy of Terry and Hilary Johnson.*

Paul's duck creations have been described as "whimsical" and seem to be of the breed found on children's amusements at the fairground. The weight has a large black foot as an integral part of the weight and a PY cane can be found in the center of the flower with heart-shaped leaves. This paperweight would make a magical gift for a favorite grandchild, and what an investment it may become for the future.

Parrot Paperweight, Paul Ysart. Dia. 3", Height 2". $1200/1500. *Courtesy of Terry and Hilary Johnson.*

A lifelike representation of a colorful parrot sitting on a branch with green foliage and a PY cane. The bird is framed over a red and white spattered ground and contrasts nicely with the green and blue bird. Paul made quite a few variations of parrots while at Caithness, and although at first glance they may look alike, on closer inspection they all have subtle color differences, or rest on a different type of tree branch, each one an individual work of art.

Basket Posy Paperweight, Paul Ysart. Dia. 2.8", Height 2". $1100/ 1300. *Courtesy of Terry and Hilary Johnson.*

This beautiful signed posy in a basket is almost identical to posy weights made by Paul at Moncrieff's 20 to 30 years previous to the making of this weight, but the infrared test puts it firmly in the Caithness period, with the glass fluorescing in the same way as all the other weights in this chapter

Flower and Bud Paperweight, Paul Ysart. Dia. 2.8, Height 2". **$600/800.** *Courtesy of Terry and Hilary Johnson.*

This paperweight fluoresces in the same colors as the previous examples of Paul's work from his Caithness years, but this was a commonly made subject throughout his career. This weight has been constructed with the utmost skill and care, and is perfect in every way. The stave basket of white spiral canes reach half way into the dome to frame the flower in a network of lace.

Crown Paperweight, Paul Ysart. Dia. 2.75", Height 1.8". $350/ 500. *Courtesy of Roy and Pam Brown.*

Crown weights were made in profusion and variety and were rarely signed. The identifying mark was a paper label reading, "PY Made in Scotland" stuck to the base. Many of these weights were sold through the Caithness shop attached to the visitor center, and were priced around $25 each.

Crown Paperweight, Paul Ysart. Dia. 2.75", Height 1.8". $350/500. *Courtesy of Roy and Pam Brown.*

Crown Paperweight, Paul Ysart. Dia. 2.75", Height 1.8". $350/500. *Courtesy of Roy and Pam Brown.*

Crown Paperweight, Paul Ysart. Dia. 2.75", Height 1.8". $350/500. *Courtesy of Roy and Pam Brown.*

Crown Paperweight, Paul Ysart. Dia. 2.75", Height 1.8". $350/500. *Courtesy of Roy and Pam Brown.*

In 1970, near the end of Paul's stay with Caithness, he became involved with Colin Terris the chief designer at Caithness in the production of millifiori jewelry. The small canes made by Paul were set in sterling silver mounts and became an instant success. These canes were inserted into many items including earrings, rings, cuff links, tie pins and pendants.

Rings, Paul Ysart. $75/100. *Courtesy of Terry and Hilary Johnson.*

Pendants, Paul Ysart. $75/100. *Courtesy of Terry and Hilary Johnson.*

Box, Paul Ysart. $200. *Courtesy of Terry and Hilary Johnson.*

Rings, Paul Ysart. $75/100. *Courtesy of Terry and Hilary Johnson.*

CHAPTER 8

EDINBURGH CRYSTAL, FOUNDED IN 1867

Penicuik, Scotland

Edinburgh Crystal has played a proud part in the history and production of Scottish glass, and in particular glassmaking in the Edinburgh area. For over three centuries, glass has been made within the city walls of Edinburgh. First, in the Citadel in the port area of Leith, and, last, in the Norton Park area of the city. Presently Edinburgh Crystal occupies a custom-built factory 10 miles south of the city in the small town of Penicuik.

Glass produced in the 1600s in Leith was mainly a variety of bottles and drinking glasses of commercial quality. By the end of the following century, fine crystal and window glass was being made that was comparable to anything imported from Europe. During the 19th century, the crystal production of Leith and its neighboring area of Portobello (which had only briefly made crystal in the 1830s and 1840s) went into a steep decline. This loss of crystal production was more than compensated for by the increasing demand for bottles. Both glass producers were soon concentrating on meeting the huge demand for bottles by the brewers and distilleries in Scotland.

In the early part of the 19th century, fine hand-made crystal was produced in Edinburgh and in particular at John Ford's glass house, which later became known as The Royal Holyrood Glassworks. This firm was known for its cut and engraved crystal, and also for its colored glass and novelties, such as paperweights. The Ford glass house was to close down, eventually, in 1904, which left The Edinburgh and Leith glassworks based in the Norton Park area of the city, as the sole producer of crystal glass in the city.

The very name Edinburgh Crystal is synonymous with fine glass and engraving worldwide, but, strangely, having identified a gap in their product range, the workforce did not possess the necessary skills to make paperweights of a quality fine enough to complement the range of products in the company's catalog at the time. As many of the company's wholesale and retail outlets were asking for paperweights to fill this gap in their range, the company had a choice of setting up and training a workforce to make weights or of contracting out the production.

The decision was made to offer the contract to Caithness Glass, who eventually made fine paperweights for the company, signed with a letter E cane to denote Edinburgh Crystal. This cane can be found in all weights sold by the company in the concentrics and range of lampworked pieces. The date of this outside production was 1986 to 1987 and was included in the company's catalog of those years. Several thousands of weights were made in two production runs and all were sold.

Many were sold through the company's own retail shop on the factory site and are well remembered by the shop manager, Kathy Boyle, and by Danny Fair, the senior designer. Danny has been working at Edinburgh Crystal for 38 years and has seen many friggers produced by the workforce using colored glass. However, the company's only official weights are solid clear glass with engraved decorations. Edinburgh Crystal had withdrawn from the paperweight market by 1990 to concentrate on the product sectors of wine suites, barware and traditional hollowware and giftware, in which they remain market leaders. Thus leaving the paperweight market to the specialist makers.

Every year thousands of visitors arrive from all over the world to visit the gift shop that showcases the extensive range of glassware made by the company, and to experience glassmaking at first hand on a conducted tour of the glassworks, preceded by a video presentation and exhibition.

The Edinburgh Crystal Factory, Penicuik, Near Edinburgh, Scotland.

Edinburgh Crystal can be found in a factory a few miles outside Edinburgh. This is a very large facility designed specifically to cater to the visitor and the tourist trade that frequents the area at all times of the year. Parking for car and bus passengers is very extensive and right next to the factory.

The Entrance to The Visitor Centre.

A page from the catalog issued in 1986, showing the full range of paperweights available from Edinburgh Crystal.

A comprehensive range of weights were made for Edinburgh Crystal and some have become desirable collector weights. The Bohemian Butterfly in particular, shows a very pretty and lifelike interpretation of the winged insect. Flashed in translucent green glass and faceted, the butterfly hovers over a swirling colored ground; with only 100 made, I would anticipate an auction price of $500/700 and maybe more.

Portrait of the Co-Founder Alexander Jenkinson. Also shown are photographs of Edinburgh Crystal's First Retail Shop at 10, Princes Street, Edinburgh; The Glass House At Norton Park in The 1950s; and The Works Parade in 1926.

As you arrive at the visitor center entrance hall, these four historic, sepia photographs stand out in the very modern center and reception area which is the meeting place and start of the factory tour.

Five Row Concentric Edinburgh Crystal Paperweight. *Courtesy of Edinburgh Crystal.*

A very extensive array of crystal is available from the company's showroom.

This paperweight is the only weight available at the factory for photographing. The piece was being used for its intended purpose, holding down papers on the shop manager's desk. Made by Caithness Glass for Edinburgh Crystal to offer through its many retail outlets, the paperweight was identifiable by an E cane. In this weight the cane can be seen in the center. The value of this piece would be around $200/300 because of the quite rare E cane.

EDINBURGH CRYSTAL   81

EDINBURGH PAPERWEIGHTS

Paperweights have long been objects of delight to committed collectors and amateur enthusiasts alike. Their appeal lies in the infinite variety of colours, designs and textures available in the medium of glass. Early designs, which can mainly be traced back to mid 19th Century France, are now much sought after and command very respectable prices at top international sales.

The 1986 range of Edinburgh paperweights includes fascinating new introductions and both limited and unlimited pieces.

Bohemian Butterfly
E686 — 85093 Edition size: 100

Flower of Scotland
E687 — 85094 Edition size: 100

Amber Ambience
E689 — 85096 Edition size: 250

Aquamarine
E652 — 85012 Edition size: 250

Highland Heather
E690 — 85097 Edition size: 250

Turquoise Delight
E654 — 85014 Edition size: 500

Thistle
E688 — 85095 Edition size: 250

Staccato
E691 — 85098 Edition size: 500

Loveheart
E692 — 85099 Edition size: 500

Opaline Garden
E653 — 85013 Edition size: 500

Evening Dew
E655 — 85015 Unlimited

Ring of Roses
E656 — 85016 Unlimited

Lilac Vine
E657 — 85017 Unlimited

Wheel of Fortune
E693 — 85100 Unlimited

Lodestar
E694 — 85101 Unlimited

Rock Candy
E658 — 85018 Unlimited

Bed of Cane
E659 — 85019 Unlimited

Spring Meadow
E695 -- 85102 Unlimited

CHAPTER 9

SELKIRK GLASS LTD, FOUNDED 1977

Selkirk, Scotland

Beside the trout and salmon filled River Ettrick, in the beautiful Borders area of Scotland, stands the custom built Selkirk Glasshouse. The welcoming visitor center plays host to many tourists and travelers to this enchanting part of Scotland. The small town of Selkirk is set among rolling hills and impressive pine and scree covered valleys, in this quiet and inspiring area of natural beauty. The gift shop covers a wide range of Scottish products and paperweights, with the added bonus of a fully stocked restaurant which can seat a hundred people, where you can dine and watch through large glass windows the activities of the paperweight makers.

Peter Holmes and Ron Hutchinson were the inspiration behind Selkirk Glass. First they set up a small glass house in a workshop rented from the local Council, in Linglie Mill, an old paper mill and warehouse alongside the river in Selkirk. The partners also had help from Peter's brother Philip and a lady polisher. The firm was established to make paperweights for the gift trade and collector market.

However, the story of Selkirk Glass stretches much further back in time to a chance encounter with Paul Ysart, who in 1962 had met 15-year-old Peter Holmes, at the blacksmith's shop in the village of Gillock. Paul Ysart at this time was the training officer for Caithness Glass, and, in January 1963, Paul invited the young Peter Holmes to join him at Caithness as an apprentice glass blower under his direction. Peter's paperweight making progressed slowly at first as Paul Ysart was very protective of his glassmaking secrets, which had been passed down through several generations of family glassblowers. Paul Ysart was so protective of his hard learned skills that at this time he only made paperweights on weekends and after the other workers had gone home for the evening. Peter Holmes had been chosen by Paul Ysart as a young man with a skillful touch. Paul invited Peter to assist him in the making of some of the more delicate pieces and lampwork, but before he would allow Peter to begin work, he insisted that he sign a document that was designed to stop Peter from disclosing any of the secrets that had been learned from the master. Peter related this story to me with regret that he did not get a copy of the document concerned, as these many years later it would be of considerable interest to himself and would have given an insight into the secretive world of the master craftsmen of paperweight making.

During the day, master and pupil would be involved in general glassmaking, but on weekends the pair of glassmakers entered a world of their own. Using all of his inherited and self-taught skills, the old man, assisted by the boy created paperweights of a most exquisite and artistic nature. Among the weights made during this period were Salamander and Snake designs. Paul was the maker, with Peter there as assistant only. Peter was a quick learner and one Sunday afternoon, after work had finished for the day, and Paul had gone home, Peter was left to clean up and tidy for the next day's work. The young man noticed there was still a small amount of glass left in the pot. Peter decided to have a go at making a snake weight on his own. The snake weight he produced that afternoon was a personal triumph for the fledgling paperweight maker. He succeeded with a very passable weight, at his first try. Pleased with his endeavors, he showed the weight to Paul Ysart the next morning. Paul became angry and took the weight from the youngster on the pretense that he would show it to his wife May.

That was the last Peter ever saw of that weight. He says Paul was angry because Peter had managed to create a passable interpretation of a snake at his first attempt. The weight in question has never been seen since that day, but Peter would recognize the weight, as it had a forked tongue protruding from its mouth, drooping down over its bottom jaw. Paul Ysart's snake weights never included a tongue because of this sagging problem, so if anyone still has that weight, Peter would like to buy it back.

During his time with Caithness Glass, Peter would use up any glass left at the end of a shift to experiment with abstract designs in paperweights. While perfecting these techniques, he came to the attention of the chief designer Colin Terris. Terris recognized the commercial implications of the abstract weights and between the two of them they produced a wide range of designs to go into paperweights that could be produced in large volumes. Paul Ysart never showed any interest at the time in abstract weights, although Peter once heard Paul remark that one of his abstract weights was "nice" and he did like it, and could he have it as a keepsake. This was indeed high praise from the master, who kept the weight next to his telephone at home for many years.

In 1972, Paul Ysart left Caithness Glass to start his own glass house, but at this time Paul and Peter had been making enlarged canes that were incorporated into a very successful range of jewelry items. Realizing that the only man left capable of continuing with the jewelry line was Peter Holmes, the company quickly secured Peter's services for the future with an offer of his own department and a significant salary increase, all of which was much appreciated by a newly married Peter Holmes. Despite running his own department, Peter yearned to express his artistic talents as had Paul Ysart. In 1977, he left the employment of Caithness Glass along with the then sales manager Ron Hutchinson, who would add valuable sales experience to this new venture to start in their own right as paperweight makers.

Ron Hutchinson's sales experience took them to their first large Trade & Gift Show at the National Exhibition Centre in Birmingham in 1978. I was also a visitor to that same show and purchased an abstract undersea paperweight from their stand. This show was a turning point in the company's future. So many orders were taken for their abstract weights that they were unsure of meeting the demand. A whole year's production was sold to the "Fine Gift" trades from that one show. Deciding to take a gamble, Peter and Ron took on two more assistants and a former apprentice from Caithness who had worked with Peter. David McGregor and Peter's brother Philip Holmes, who were both experienced paperweight makers of some note, were a welcome addition to the firm.

Peter had remained in contact with his old teacher Paul Ysart, and when Paul rang to say that David Hurry, his main assistant at his own small glassworks, Paul Ysart Glass Ltd, near Wick, had left at very short notice, Peter promptly loaned him one of his own apprentices, to help out the ageing Paul Ysart while he tried to recruit another worker. This was a magnanimous gesture by Peter, who still held his old teacher in high esteem, but it was not enough to keep the master going. At aged 79 years Paul Ysart decided to retire permanently.

Peter and Ron bought all the workshop equipment from Paul and agreed to sell for him his stock of paperweights that were unsold at the time of his retirement. There were 240 Harlequin and Fountains and approximately 100 signed weights of various types. Peter and Ron "cherry picked" the best of these weights for their own private collections and agreed to sell for Paul the remainder through their shop at Selkirk Glass. In a short time they had sold about 180 of these weights, but Paul was growing impatient for his money and took away the remaining weights to sell himself. Paul sold the rest off through local gift shops. The asking price for these weights at the time was £2.50 Sterling or $4 US, each. Several years later, Paul Ysart sold his working tools to a craftsman at the Selkirk Glassworks named James Mcbeath who regularly uses the tools to make weights. We hope this craftsman uses the tools to reach the heights that Paul achieved.

The Selkirk Glass Company now concentrates on the domestic and export trades, with nearly half of all production being exported. Important markets being developed by the sales team are to the USA, Germany, and in particular France, the traditional home of quality paperweight making.

Most of the glass batch comes from an original Paul Ysart recipe handed down to Peter by Paul Ysart with hardly any change in formula. Peter and Ron have recently taken on a production manager to allow them more time from the day-to-day business to develop and create innovative designs and expand into new areas of paperweight-making. At present Peter creates approximately twenty paperweights and inkwells weekly, all of collector quality, as well as special commissions. Selkirk Glass paperweights can be seen in many museums including Perth Museum, Victoria and Albert Museum, London, Edinburgh City Museum, and Kelvingrove Museum and Art Gallery, Glasgow.

Selkirk Glass Ltd, Selkirk, Scotland.

The Borders Region of Scotland is a delightful area of outstanding natural beauty that incorporates several small market towns, including Moffat and Selkirk, and as an added attraction the Selkirk Glass visitor center. Easily found on the outskirts of this small town, a warm welcome awaits anyone visiting the area on vacation or with paperweights in mind.

The Raw Materials Needed to Make a Paperweight.

On entering Selkirk Glass visitor center, the first display case features some of the raw materials needed to make a paperweight and samples of the finished products.

Opposite page:
The Scottish Borders Region.

The Viewing Gallery.

Visitors can get close to the action and feel the heat in this glassworks. The workers go about their business but someone is always available to answer questions.

Peter Holmes inspecting paperweights before being dispatched worldwide.

Peter checks on the final polishing before sanctioning dispatch. His attention to the smallest detail makes sure no weights leave the factory with imperfections.

A fine display from the Selkirk Glass paperweight makers.

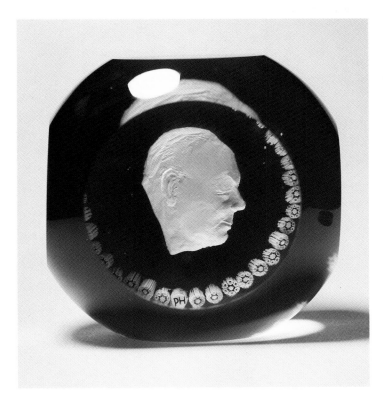

Winston Churchill Sulphide Paperweight, Peter Holmes. $1200.
Courtesy of Selkirk Glass.

This is a one-off paperweight made by Peter Holmes at the start of Selkirk Glass in 1977. The weight is signed with a bold PH signature cane and was made as a test piece, and never offered for sale. A garland of green and white complex canes frames a sulphide of Great Britain's war time Prime Minister. During the following year a selection of sulphide paperweights were on offer from Selkirk Glass.

Fruit Paperweight, Peter Holmes. 1979. $450/550. *Courtesy of Selkirk Glass.*

A wide variety of paperweights were made from the start by Peter Holmes and included modern and traditional styles. Throughout the company's existence they have made more abstract weights than the more time consuming millefiori and lampwork pieces; and this is still the case today. Peter is responsible for the more technically difficult lampwork and millefiori pieces, and as he trained under Paul Ysart, his work is of the highest order and workmanship. This fruit weight was made in a limited edition of 200 and includes a selection of grapes, oranges, apples and a peach. The fruit has a covering of tiny bubbles due to oxidixation of the surface material when the hot covering dome of glass was lowered over the fruit.

Robert Burns Sulphide Paperweight, Peter Holmes. 1978. $450/550. *Courtesy of Selkirk Glass.*

This sulphide weight was made to sell through the shop on the premises of Linglie Mill, Selkirk, where the glassworks were situated in the early years of this company. The weight has a single blue flash overlay, which is then faceted to reveal the subject. Robbie Burns is a favorite subject of glassmakers, and this piece was made in an edition of 250 and sold out quickly.

A large posy of flowers made in a style similar to Peter's former tutor Paul Ysart. In the early years of his own glass house we see new styles being developed at Selkirk but with a memory of his earlier years showing in Peter's work. This inkwell is superbly made and although the posy may look like Paul's work the bottle design is certainly a Selkirk piece.

Made in a limited edition of 450, this multi-petaled red rose is stunningly beautiful. The weight sits on a crystal foot and has the added attraction of side facets and a top window to view this lovely creation. Each paperweight is handmade individually, which ensures that two pieces are never identically the same.

Saturn Paperweight, Peter Holmes. 1981. $450-550.
Courtesy of Selkirk Glass.

This abstract weight has a totally realistic look with the flat rings of Saturn held by gravitational pull in the depths of space. The large window allows one to gaze deep into imagination.

Wild Rose Paperweight, Peter Holmes. 1982. $550-700. *Courtesy of Selkirk Glass.*

A botanically perfect representation of a wild rose and hips. Commonly called the Dog Rose, this flower can be seen in hedgerows everywhere at the beginning of the summer. The pure white coloring of the petals, tinged with red, adds realism to the design. The center of the rose has a stamen made from tiny dark millefiori rods that look extremely life-like and make the paperweight very special. A lovely weight to view and a collector's dream to own.

Abstract Pegasus Paperweight, Peter Holmes. 1983. $300. *Courtesy of Selkirk Glass.*

The design in this weight shows an upward twisting swirl of movement as though caught in a vortex. The paperweight has a lovely arrangement of blue coloring that is precisely set to capture the upward movement of the translucent Pegasus wings.

Christmas Rose Paperweight, Peter Holmes. 1985. $550-650. *Courtesy of Selkirk Glass.*

This lovely paperweight in an edition of only 75 pieces has all the colors of a traditional Christmas. Red berries on green prickly holly leaves, and a pure white Christmas rose as a focal point. The rose has a stamen made of bright yellow very small rods in its center, which looks striking against the pure white of the petals. The set-up sits in a pale green and white spiral basket that looks light and delicate against the red and green holly. Three side facets for viewing the holly and flower with a large top window.

Bluebells Paperweight, Peter Holmes. 1984. $300-350. *Courtesy of Selkirk Glass.*

A simple but elegant Bluebell plant with tall leaves and flower heads set against a star cut base. A spaced garland of large millefiori canes frames the central feature, with the paperweight having six side facets and a large viewing window. Made in an edition size of 250.

Basket of Flowers Paperweight, Peter Holmes. 1986. $550-650.
Courtesy of Selkirk Glass.

A white latticinio basket frames these pink flowers. The basket is formed by placing latticinio rods in a grooved mold to hold them in place, while the gather of glass is gently lowered into the center of the mold to which the outside row of rods adheres which can then be removed and shaped. It sounds quite simple but can result in movement of the rods and subsequent untidiness in the final appearance. In this weight the procedure went according to plan and is perfectly formed to frame a desirable set-up of flowers.

Halleys Comet Paperweight, Peter Holmes. 1986. $300.
Courtesy of Selkirk Glass.

This weight was made in an edition of 500 and sold out. As with millefiori and lampworked paperweights, abstract and modernistic weights are seriously collected worldwide with certain pieces changing hands for thousands of dollars. This piece shows the earth with Halley's comet flying by with the tail clearly seen against the infinite backdrop of space.

Summer Bouquet Paperweight, Peter Holmes. 1988. $500-600.*Courtesy of Selkirk Glass.*

Four large clematis flowers lie on a bed of leaves, which rests on a green ground made from spattered glass chippings to add contrast to the vibrant colors of the flowers. The weight was made in an edition of 100 only and, as with almost all of Peter Holmes's creations, completely sold out quickly. Most of the paperweights made by Selkirk Glass vary only marginally in size with an average diameter around 3.25". Each paperweight always comes in an attractive box and has a certificate of authenticy.

This bottle and complementary weight was made in an edition of 150 in this undersea abstract pattern, but Peter also makes the bottles with lampworked flowers within the design. These sets are extremely attractive and are eagerly sought by collectors. All Peter's work has his PH cane embedded within the design.

Summertime Paperweight, Peter Holmes. 1991. $650-750.
Courtesy of Selkirk Glass.

A superbly made dragonfly, with a long tapering body and translucent blue and clear wings. It hovers over a large water lily. The lily has its stamen made from several hundreds of tapered yellow rods, which are set between the thick waxy petals of this lovely flower. The whole flower rests on a bed of leaves that float on a blue pond. The edition size was only 75 pieces.

Daffodils Paperweight, Peter Holmes. 1996. $325/ 375. *Courtesy of Selkirk Glass.*

This attractive daffodil weight sits on a bed of scrambled lace canes with an outer garland of spaced complex canes to frame the central feature. The daffodil has a yellow realistic trumpet and white petals, with two unopened flowers coming through.

Flower Paperweight, Peter Holmes. 1995. $150/175. *Courtesy of Selkirk Glass.*

Selkirk Glass tries to cater to all sections of the collector and gift markets. The price this paperweight was sold for through the company's outlets seems to have hit the mark. Made in a limited edition of 100, the weight was quickly sold out. A simple red flower and leaves sit on a dark background with a spaced millefiori garland to frame the design. A superbly made piece at a budget price and with a PH cane.

Bouquet Anniversary Paperweight, Peter Holmes. 1997. $750. *Courtesy of Selkirk Glass.*

A magnificent bouquet of flowers, stunningly set on a blue flashed ground. The clematis type flowers have striped leaves. The pink flower has petals made from a stretched cog cane to create the veins in the petals. The centers of the flowers are complex millefiori and tiny bundled rods make the stamens. The four flowers have leaves and six more buds await emerging into bloom. The bouquet is framed with an unusual array of latticinio rods and millefiori canes formed into two rows around the perimeter. The complexity of the paperweight meant that only twenty were made in this limited edition. The weight has Peter's PH cane sitting proudly near the bottom of the design.

Pansy and Bud Paperweight, Peter Holmes. 1998. $450. *Courtesy of Selkirk Glass.*

This lovely pansy weight is not in Selkirk's catalog for 1998 and was produced in small numbers, as samples. The flower rests within a stave basket, which has a row of complex canes around the top to garland the paperweight. Signed with a PH cane in the garland.

Opposite page:
Stargazer Anniversary Paperweight, Peter Holmes. 1997. $75/100. *Courtesy of Selkirk Glass.*

A production of approximately 200 were made to commemorate twenty years in business, which in itself is an achievement. Celebrated with this abstract design of uncountable millefiori stars in an infinite universe, it has a symbolism which reflects the ambitions of the company. The paperweight has Peter's PH cane on the colored ground.

Bouquet Paperweight, Peter Holmes. 1998. $750. *Courtesy of Selkirk Glass.*

Peter Holmes at Work. 1998.

Much of Peters time is taken up with managerial responsibilities, which restricts the time he has to make paperweights. But he has said that he intends to spend more time designing and making weights in the future. The composition and content found in this weight is an example that will make collectors everywhere anxious and waiting for Peter's new creations to appear.

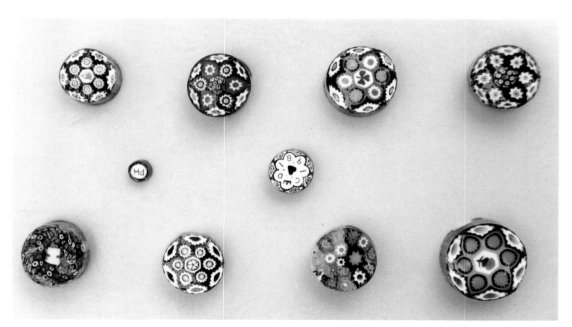

Close up of complex canes by Peter Holmes. *Courtesy of Selkirk Glass.*

Among these very complex canes can be found a Scottish thistle, clover leaf and a daffodil, all as the centers of composite canes. The two signature canes PH and H have both been placed in weights by Peter Holmes. The single H was used only rarely in the earlier years to avoid confusion with paperweights being made at the Harland glassworks by Paul Ysart, which were also signed with a H cane. Peter now only uses the PH to identify his weights.

CHAPTER 10

CAITHNESS GLASS LTD, FOUNDED 1961

Perth, Scotland

Established in 1961 in the small town of Wick, in Scotland's most northerly county, Caithness Glassworks did not produce paperweights until 1969 with the exception of weights that were made by Paul Ysart who had joined the company in 1963. As training officer, Paul was only allowed to make weights on weekends and at the end of a workshift. His weights were occasionally sold through the company shop and all were unsigned except for paperweights made for Paul Jokelson an American collector and dealer, which were signed with a PY cane and exported to the USA. Paperweights were made in the Wick glassworks until 1983, at which time all paperweight production was transferred to the Perth works.

It would be right to say that the founding father of Caithness paperweights was Colin Terris, who had joined the company in 1968 to set up an engraving and design studio. Only after being introduced to Paul Ysart, and watching him make paperweights on the weekend, did it occur to Colin that here was an art form that he could develop and expand into abstract styles that would meet the needs of the gift trade that Caithness so relied upon. With the help of Paul's assistant Peter Holmes, Terris experimented with all manner of designs within the crystal ball of glass. He was sufficiently encouraged at an early stage by these first efforts in abstract designs in paperweights to continue further. Terris realized that he was the first to try this technique, which did not use traditional millefiori or lampwork to decorate the inside of a weight. He set about designing a set of four paperweights that he called the Planets. Issued in a limited edition of 500, with 400 going to the USA, the edition was sold out very quickly, bought by a collecting public that was fascinated by the unusual abstract designs encased in a glass dome. At the same time as the planets were made, an order from Harrods in London had been received to coincide with the imminent moon landing. The weights were produced and awaited engraving, which was to take place as soon as the landing had been successfully achieved. The date was July 21, 1969, and the weights were quickly engraved and dispatched with haste to Harrods in London. The entire exclusive edition was sold out within days of the landing.

Over the years many hundreds of designs have been made to great acclaim for this innovative style which has made Caithness the largest producer of quality paperweights in the world. Many great paperweight makers have contributed down the years with their own artful designs. Among them are Paul Ysart, Colin Terris, Allan Scott, Peter Holmes and Willie Manson. Many experimental pieces have been made, including a five-color overlay that proved too risky to put into production due to technical problems. The overlay was reduced to a four-color overlay in 1995 and called Caribbean Sunrise, which was limited to 25 pieces. Caithness weights made from the beginning in 1969 are signed on the base. But in 1983 Caithness began to mark all unlimited production weights with a prefix letter starting with A for 1983, B for 1984, C for 1985 and so on. This is still being carried on today with the letter R for 1999. If for instance you have a Moonflower paperweight in your collection marked C 206, this would mean that the paperweight was made in 1985 and was the 206th paperweight made so far that year; not that it was the 206th Moonflower made that year. This code applies for all unlimited paperweights made by Caithness.

Caithness collectors are part of a club that was formed in 1976 by Colin Terris, and is recognized as one of the first collecting societies established in the field of china and glass. The Caithness Collectors Society stretches worldwide and reaches 12,000 accredited and active members who wait patiently for each yearly limited edition, made exclusively for club members.

In 1981 Caithness bought the Whitefriars name, tools, color formulae, and records from the Official Receiver after the Whitefriars Glass Company had ceased trading, due to a shortage of orders. Fearing that this 300-year-old name might be lost to a foreign competitor, Caithness quickly stepped in and now issue a yearly Whitefriars limited edition paperweight, with the Whitefriars logo of a white monk enclosed within the design.

Caithness Glass produces paperweights that are sold in over 1,400 outlets in the UK alone, and are exported to 48 countries. The company employs around 275 people spread through the three factories. A new factory was built at Wick in 1992 and now produces all the holloware, blown glass and engraved pieces offered by the company. The Oban factory is now a visitor center and factory shop, with the main glass-making facility in the district of Inveralmond on the outskirts of Perth, where a large visitor center and factory shop caters to many thousands of tourists every year who are able to see, at first hand, the skills needed to produce these wonderful objects. The center also has a permanent display of the company's products, including most of the paperweights produced from 1969 to the present day.

The original Caithness factory at Wick, Scotland. *Courtesy of Caithness Glass Ltd.*

In 1961 Caithness was founded in the most northerly county of Scotland. A mainly rural area with a coastline of outstanding beauty on sunny and temperate days but wild and dramatic when the wind turns northerly, and blows hard from the not-too-distant Arctic. The factory brought much needed work to the area and traditional local skills were quickly utilized to begin producing tableware and decorative items.

Moonflowers. $75-100. *Courtesy of Caithness Glass Ltd.*

This series of unlimited but inspiring paperweights named "Moonflowers" were designed by Colin Terris and heralded in an era of paperweight production that spans thirty years. These paperweights are still being made today at Caithness, and are considered to be the world's largest selling paperweight having been produced in many thousands and still remains a popular gift paperweight. The use of bubbles with abstract designs has fascinated collectors and the public since their inception in 1969. The question, *"How do they get the bubbles in the glass?"* must have been posed thousands of times.

Caithness Glass Plc. Inveralmond, Perth, Scotland. *Courtesy of Caithness Glass Ltd.*

In 1983, all paperweight production was moved to the Perth factory, which had a greater capacity for producing the very significant volumes that were required by the high quality gifts trade, and an increasing membership of the collectors club, who demanded a new limited edition, exclusive to them, annually. This glassworks is now firmly established on the Scottish tourist route for serious collectors and the general public alike. Tourists are well catered to in the large gift shop and restaurant with superb displays of paperweights and glassware and guided tours of the glassworks available all year round.

Next page:
Limited Edition Abstract Paperweights. $250/550. *Courtesy of Caithness Glass Ltd.*

A carousel, swirls, bubbles, ribbons and stunning design can all be viewed within these glass baubles. All are designed to stimulate and inspire the imagination of the viewer. Colin Terris spends hours on the factory floor, practicing the many different techniques required to produce this type of paperweight in order to get it right before he allows his talented glassworkers to start a production run.

Shangri-La. Limited Edition of 150. $350/ 450. *Courtesy of Caithness Glass Ltd.*

Issued in 1987 for $150, the prices of Caithness paperweights show steady appreciation, and provide a greater opportunity to acquire a collector's piece in comparison with most other paperweight producers. In this weight, traditional faceting enhances the ultramodern interior design. Flashed with a hint of green the brown earth and bubbles have rings of silver floating above the ground.

Previous page:
Modern Limited Edition. $400/500. *Courtesy of Caithness Glass Ltd.*

A large facet opens the way to the interior design that has white ribbon spiralling around the twisted bright yellow core. The base has a dark blue flash to add further to the beauty of this paperweight.

Opposite page:
Elements 2. Limited Edition of 250. $500/750. *Courtesy of Caithness Glass* Ltd.

The second Elements set of paperweights designed by Colin Terris were issued in 1989 as a boxed presentation set of four weights, to celebrate 20 years of paperweight making. In an edition of 250, they were quickly sold, as were the first Elements, which had an edition size of 1000 and also sold out.

Jupiter Limited Edition of 750. $200/250. *Courtesy of Caithness Glass Ltd.*

This was Caithness's interpretation of Jupiter and its moons, Gannymede and Io, as seen from the North American Space Agency photograph. The weight was issued in 1987 after the fly by at a cost of only $60.These topical weights were quickly snapped up.

Jubilee Orchid. Collectors Club Exclusive Paperweight. *Courtesy of Caithness Glass Ltd.*

Issued in 1994, the annual collector's limited edition piece, is eagerly awaited by the members, with the edition size restricted to the number of orders taken by a certain date. These collector paperweights and the annual edition of Reflections, the collectors own magazine, keeps club members well informed of developments, trends and news stories. As a member of this club, you are encouraged to attend one of the regular paper-weight conventions held at Perth,where members get together from all over the world, to meet and interchange ideas and views on paperweights.

**1997 Caithness Glass Collectors Paper-
weight Convention, Perth Scotland.
*Courtesy of Caithness Glass Ltd.***

At the 1997 convention, delegates are
shown around the glassworks to view
paperweights in all stages of construction. A
fascinating and instructional experience for
all concerned.

**Caribbean Sunrise. Limited Edition of 25,
Quadruple Overlay. $1000/1200. *Courtesy
of Caithness Glass Ltd.***

The design and execution of this magnificent
paperweight brings to mind white sands,
crystal blue seas and a warm tropical sunrise.
The first attempt to make this weight entailed
no less than five different colored overlays but
because of production difficulties this was
reduced to four. Inspired design by Colin
Terris has allowed the master glassmakers of
Caithness to express themselves to their
fullest ability; using 35 years of learning that
goes back to Paul Ysart as training officer in
1963. Issued in 1995, this weight had a retail
price of $750 and is only rarely seen by
collectors with only one, known by the
author, to be offered for sale at auction since
the edition was taken up.

Back View of Caribbean Sunrise. *Courtesy of Terry and Hilary Johnson.*

The rear view is almost as stunning as the front. The overlays of glass can be seen to their most dramatic effect. Very deeply cut to reveal the four colors of the overlaying glass, which could tempt you to display the paperweight in this position.

25th Anniversary Paperweight. Edition of 25. *Courtesy of Caithness Glass Ltd.*

In 1994 Caithness decided to issue an anniversary weight to celebrate 25 years of paperweight making. They did it in a big way with this 4 kilogram (9 pounds) Double Magnum, multi-faceted abstract weight. The size of this piece is about the maximum a glassworker can handle.

Sunset Orchid. Limited Edition of 100. $500/600. *Courtesy of Caithness Glass Ltd.*

This Colin Terris design was the forerunner to Caribbean Sunrise. Here this weight shows a light orange flash overlay that has a large window facet cut to reveal the delicate orchid within. Issued in 1992, it was fully subscribed by a collecting fraternity that was eager to purchase a weight that had traditional Caithness internal design, and innovation in its coloring and faceting.

Alley Cat and Small World. *Courtesy of Caithness Glass Ltd.*

These two whimsical paperweights demonstrate the techniques of engraving to enhance the paperweight design. The cat sits contentedly gazing down a long alleyway that has views of houses with windows with the alleyway tapering off into the distance. A large window facet allows a view inside the weight which has been ground to a matte finish on the outside. The gold fish swim contentedly around the bowl that has water weed and fronds deeply engraved on the outside. True innovation from the world's largest producer of quality paperweights.

Dinosaurs Unlimited Editions issued in 1998. $100/150. *Courtesy of Caithness Glass Ltd.*

These inexpensive weights make great gifts for the kids, with good representations of the ever popular Dinosaurs and Pterodactyls made from powdered glass. A nice introduction to collecting paperweights for the youngsters.

Limited Editions issued in 1998. $300/500.
Courtesy of Caithness Glass Ltd.

This selection of limited editions shows the variety available every year to the serious collector. Many different shapes and designs are available with or without facets, and in a multitude of colors.

Collectible Eggs. *Courtesy of Caithness Glass Ltd.*

Caithness introduced something new to their range in 1998 that may prove to be as addictive as paperweight collecting. Crystal and ornamental eggs have been produced for centuries and have been collected for almost as long. In the mid-19th century, glass eggs were used as hand coolers and made by Baccarat, Clichy and the Saint Louis glassworks. Probably the most famous and expensive are the gold and jeweled eggs made for the Russian Czars in the 18th and 19th centuries by Fabergé, jewelers to the Royal Court. These very rare pieces can fetch enormous sums of money, which reflect the artistry and value of the gold and diamonds set into them. Caithness pieces are not quite so expensive but could prove to be an area of collecting that may grow significantly, as more and more glass houses and artists produce their own versions of Fabergé's eggs.

Whitefriars Zodiac. Edition of 250. $500/600. *Courtesy of Caithness Glass Ltd.*

In 1983, Caithness began to issue millefiori paperweights in the Whitefriars tradition. Now that Caithness owns the name and 300 molds, tools, millefiori rods and glass formulas plus the company's records, of all limited editions ever made by Whitefriars, a decision was made to issue annual limited editions with the Whitefriars logo included within the weights. This Greek Zodiac weight was one of the first to be made and sold for $150. The paperweight contains twelve silhouettes, and proved to be a very difficult weight to make, as it was overlayed with alternate pink and white filigree rods and then faceted.

Whitefriars Woodland Glade. Edition of 25. $1200/1500.
Courtesy of Caithness Glass Ltd.

The Whitefriar tradition of using only millefiori canes in their designs was broken with the addition of lampwork to the Caithness versions. This superb example has been overlayed with four different colors with window facets cut through the overlays. The base has been flashed in blue and star cut. The flowers are superbly made with two fern leaves to compliment the lampwork. The Whitefriar hooded monk logo can be seen at the bottom of the design. The original 1994 issued price of this weight was $900.

CHAPTER 11

PAUL YSART, THE HARLAND YEARS, FOUNDED 1970-75

Harland Farm, Reiss, Near Wick, Scotland

Paul Ysart was encouraged by the ex-Managing Director of Caithness Glass, Graham Brown, to participate in a new venture at this remote farm building that had once been used as a radio and early warning post by the RAF during the second World War. Brown had arranged financing for the venture from a successful local businessman he knew, Robert Gunn. Gunn was a well known civil engineering contractor whose busy company allowed him very little time to be involved in the day to day activities of the Harland Glassworks, as the company became known. Paul produced paperweights with the help of an ex-apprentice from Caithness Glass, Willie Manson. Willie had been one of Paul's star pupils from his training officer days at Caithness. Paperweights produced during the four or five years of Harland's existence usually had an H cane inserted, except for weights that were destined for the USA, which were signed with a PY cane. Paul was sending approximately 40 to 50 weights every week or so to Paul Jokelson who retained the distribution rights to Paul's work in the USA. Many of the weights with the H canes were sent to an agent in Glasgow, who called on the quality gift trade retailers in the North of England and Scotland. The weights sold via these outlets were of varying quality with most being of the Harlequin type of which Paul and Willie could make as many as 40 a day.

In 1975 the Harland Glassworks was closed amid acrimonious disputes involving the financial well being of the company. In long discussions with Robert Gunn, who had put up the finances for the whole project from its inception,

it would appear that although the company could sell every piece it made, these wonderful artistic creations were underpriced. Although all the workers involved in production were working at full capacity, which involved weekend and evening work to meet order deadlines, the books simply did not balance. Advised by his accountants, Robert Gunn decided to bring proceedings to a close, and the workforce was laid off.

Paul Ysart had been in poor health for a number of years, suffering among other things migraines and severe headaches, which had on occasion caused him to abandon work for the day. At the age of 73 he still could not give up on the one thing that had kept his mind so agile and creative; he decided to carry on alone at the deserted Harland Works. Without his main assistant, Willie Manson, who had gone back to Caithness Glass, Paul hired in David Hurry as his assistant, and continued for a short while making and selling his weights under the name of Highland Paperweights. However with failing health he eventually had to retire after his assistant left, and a replacement could not be found despite help from his old friend Peter Holmes of Selkirk Glass, who loaned Paul one of his own Selkirk apprentices to try and keep him going.

Paul Ysart's career in paperweights had begun on a slow learning curve, picking up the necessary skills from his very talented father Salvador, and expanding on these skills to take paperweight making to the outer limits of this particular art form, for which the collectors of this world are extremely grateful. Paul Ysart, the greatest exponent of paperweight making of this century, died in a Wick nursing home in 1991.

Harland Glassworks, Reiss, Near Wick, Scotland.

From this building Paul Ysart and Willie Manson produced some of the finest paperweights ever to come out of Scotland. It was here that Paul produced some of his colorful snakes, bird and animal weights. Set in an area that is remote and quiet, the two men were allowed to exploit the art of paperweight making to its limits with little interference from Robert Gunn, who was busy with his other concerns, or from Graham Brown who spent most of his time promoting the paperweights being made.

Robert and Louise Gunn, Lybster, Near Wick, Scotland.

Now retired for many years, Bert and Louise Gunn well remember the time when they financed the glass operation for Paul Ysart and Graham Brown. Knowing nothing about glass except that it was the area's main employer through the nearby Caithness Glass Company, Bert was a willing participant in a new venture that looked to have a future. After the collapse of Harland Glass the remaining stock from the factory was removed by Bert to try and recoup some of his losses. He kept several hundreds of the paperweights for many years without being too concerned about selling them, and had almost forgotten them. It was only after being approached by a Glass Museum researching the Harland years and Paul Ysart in particular that the weights again saw the light of day. The Broadfield House Glass Museum in Kingswinford, England, held an exhibition featuring Paul Ysart paperweights and purchased a large number of the paperweights owned by the Gunns to be offered for sale alongside the exhibition. The exhibition was a complete success and nearly all the weights were eventually sold. With the remaining paperweights held by the Gunns being sold off to a dealer, at last Bert and Louise recovered a large proportion of their lost investment.

Lybster Harbour, Scotland.

With the fishing industry in the Wick area virtually extinct, due to conservation and quota cuts in the European Community Fishing Policy, the young workers in the mainly rural farming community were eager to take on jobs in the large Caithness Glass factory. This harbour was once a small but busy fishing port with many boats based here.

Paul Ysart's House, Near Wick, Scotland.

Paul Ysart was a quiet very private person according to many of the glassmakers who worked with him at various times, and although he achieved a certain fame in his lifetime, he was also a modest man who was content to live in a small house in a village just outside Wick.

When a large collection of Paul Ysart's and other Scottish paperweights are tested with the ultraviolet light method, clear distinctions can be seen between Paul's earlier work and paperweights made during his years at Harland and Caithness. Paperweights made during the Harland years fluoresce pink/lilac in the long wave and gray in the short wave.

Snake Paperweight, Paul Ysart. Dia. 3", Height 2.25". $1400/1600. *Courtesy of Terry and Hilary Johnson.*

A green-and-red spotted snake rests on a sand-colored ground with head raised ready to strike out. There are a few variations of this snake which have the same style, body and pose, but different colors and grounds.

Footed Cross Paperweight, Paul Ysart. Dia. 3", Height 2.75". $1400/1600. *Courtesy of Terry and Hilary Johnson.*

A foliated cross with a pink flower and the signature cane inset below the flower head makes this a rare and interesting weight. A similar paperweight was sold in 1997, as part of the Parkington collection at Christie's of London, and realized a hammer price of $1280 plus commission. The price reflects the rising demand for Ysart paperweights, which are becoming increasingly hard to find. The main source of Ysart weights is from auction and specialist dealers in the UK and USA.

**Flower Paperweight, Paul Ysart. Dia. 2.9", Height 2".
$400/600.** *Courtesy of Terry and Hilary Johnson.*

The signature cane on paperweights made at the Harland glassworks can be found either in the dome or beneath the weight embedded in the ground. This weight, garlanded with colored spiral and latticinio strips is a typical example from the works. Made in considerable numbers, it is the most likely weight found these days. Although reasonably common, this type was still made in a meticulous manner, even with this high volume production weight, Paul Ysart did not cut corners in his work. Weights with detached leaves and detritus are rare, and it has only been in recent times that a few of the remaining stock belonging to Bert Gunn, have reached the market place. They show signs of small defects, and were held back from sale until now. Nevertheless, these weights are still very desirable and keenly sought by collectors worldwide. The base of the Harland weights can be ground perfectly flat, or slightly concave with the pontil still visible and left unground.

**Flower Paperweight, Paul Ysart. Dia. 2.9", Height 2".
$400/600.** *Courtesy of Terry and Hilary Johnson.*

A good representation of a clematis flower and leaves floats above a dark blue ground with green spiral cane around the perimeter. Signed with an H cane beneath the weight.

Flower Paperweight, Paul Ysart. Dia. 3", Height 2". $500/700. *Courtesy of Terry and Hilary Johnson.*

Not all Harland weights have a single letter as the identifying signature. In this weight the H cane is hidden within a millefiori cane at the bottom of the design, a technique used by Paul in his earlier days at Moncrieff's. The variety and color combinations used in these simple but beautifully made flowers is immense and many collectors have built up substantial collections of these single flower weights.

Flower Paperweight and Bud, Paul Ysart. Dia. 2.9", **Height 2.1". $600/800** *Courtesy of Terry and* *Hilary Johnson.*

This flower looks like a Passiflora (passion flower) because of coloring and petal shape. Inside the open petals the center of the flower is created using tiny millefiori complex canes. The bud is superbly made to look almost lifelike. Set on a spattered red and white ground, the piece is a joy to behold and a treasured piece in this collection.

Flower Paperweight, Paul Ysart. Dia. 3", Height 2.2". $400/600. *Courtesy of Terry and Hilary Johnson.*

Deeply colored leaves of purple and red stand out against the deep orange of the ground. Paul Ysart was not afraid to use strong coloring in his work, and the strong orange is toned down by the use of even stronger colors in the flower and petals. The spiral canes on the perimeter also have an even stronger orange color to subdue the ground color.

Flower Paperweight, Paul Ysart. Dia 3". Height 2". $400/600. *Courtesy of Terry and Hilary Johnson.*

As the previous weight was strong so this weight is subdued in color. Pale lilac and white brings the color down to an almost washed out appearance, but the central flower has enough color to hold the piece together. The leaves and petals have the added attraction of aventurine, which gives the weight added sparkle.

Flower Paperweight, Paul Ysart. Dia. 3", Height 2.1". $ 500/700. *Courtesy of Terry and Hilary Johnson.*

The beauty of these flower paperweights is the simple theme but with an infinite variety of color and style combinations. Every weight is virtually the same, but every one is different; it is very rare to find paperweights that are exactly alike.

Two Flower Paperweights, Paul Ysart. Archive Photo. $400/600. *Courtesy of Anne Metcalfe, Sweetbriar Gallery, Helsby, England.*

Four Flower Paperweights, Paul Ysart. Archive Photo. $400/600. *Courtesy of Anne Metcalfe, Sweetbriar Gallery, Helsby, England.*

Fish Paperweight, Paul Ysart. Dia. 2.9", Height 2". $600/800. *Courtesy of Nichola Johnson.*

Fish were a popular subject for Paul, and like the single flower head weights, he made them in many varieties and colors. This paperweight has the signature cane PY, which meant it was destined for America, but has found its way onto the English market at some point in time. Although signed PY, it was made at the Harland works and fluoresces the correct color. The garland of complex colored canes around the edge adds extra value to this particular paperweight.

Fish Paperweight, Paul Ysart. Dia. 2.9", Height 2". $600/ 800. *Courtesy of Nichola Johnson.*

This fish has a set of spaced complex canes set on the outside edge, and although many of Paul's fish look alike, small subtle differences in body shape and color make them all individuals. This weight is signed with a PY cane.

Fish Paperweight, Paul Ysart. Dia. 2.9", Height 2". $400/ 600. *Courtesy of Nichola Johnson.*

This weight has an H cane set in the sandy colored ground, with a different selection of canes around the edge to individualize it from the others.

**Fish Paperweight, Paul Ysart. Dia. 2.9", Height 2".
$400/500.** *Courtesy of Nichola Johnson.*

A slightly less expensive version of the fish weight, this
and the following weights each have a row of bubbles set
around the edge. This variety was quick to do and offered
another alternative and price range.

**Fish Paperweight, Paul Ysart. Dia. 2.9",
Height 2". $400/500.** *Courtesy of
Nichola Johnson.*

Fish Paperweight, Paul Ysart. Dia.
2.9", Height 2". $400/600.
Courtesy of Nichola Johnson.

Fish Paperweight, Paul Ysart. Dia.
2.9", Height 2". $400/600. *Courtesy
of Nichola Johnson.*

**Fish Paperweight, Paul Ysart. Dia. 3", Height 2.3".
$1100/1400.** *Courtesy of Terry and Hilary Johnson.*

This pair of fish was made at Harland but Paul also
made the same type and style of fish at Caithness Glass
during his time as training officer with that company.
The lifelike spotted sticklebacks are suspended over a
sand and rock strewn ground.

**Fish Paperweights, Paul Ysart. Dia. 3", Height
2.3". $1100/1400.** *Courtesy of Terry and Hilary
Johnson.*

As a price guide to this very much sort after
paperweight, two almost identical weights were
sold in the Parkington sale at Christie's in London
for $1100 and $1400 in April 1998.

**Salamander Paperweight, Paul Ysart. Dia. 2.7",
Height 2". $1600/1700.** *Courtesy of Terry and
Hilary Johnson.*

This green and spotted amphibian stands patiently
with both front feet on a rock in a lifelike pose, as
though about to climb it, its beady black and yellow
eyes stare intently in search for its next meal. A rare
paperweight with the PY signature cane lying on the
sandy ground.

**Posy Paperweight, Paul Ysart. Dia. 3", Height 2.1".
$700/900.** *Courtesy of Terry and Hilary Johnson.*

Spaced complex canes around the edge frame this
pretty posy weight. The five flowers are not tied
with a ribbon, which would nicely set and finish off
the posy, but this posy is set on a decorous blue and
white jasper ground to make amends.

Three Flower Posy Paperweight, Paul Ysart. Dia. 3", Height 2.1". $600/800. *Courtesy of Terry and Hilary Johnson.*

Paul Ysart made this type of posy paperweight throughout his career with hardly a change to the composition of the weight. It is only with the aid of the infrared lamp that these posy weights can be dated correctly to a particular glassworks. Paperweights made during his career at Moncrieff's, Caithness and Harland all fluoresce slightly different, due to the chemical composition of his glass batch. Although Paul Ysart hardly varied the mix during his lifetime, it is possible to determine where a paperweight was made.

Fountain Paperweight, Paul Ysart. Dia. 2.25", Height 2.75". $200/300. *Courtesy of Terry and Hilary Johnson.*

This type of fountain paperweight was made in considerable numbers by Paul and his assistants at Harland. They were made in various colors but in the same basic style.

Fountain Paperweight, Paul Ysart. Dia. 2.25", Height 2.9". $350/450. *Courtesy of Terry and Hilary Johnson.*

Even though this fountain was produced in large numbers, the prices have been steadily increasing as Paul Ysart's paperweights are gathered into museums and private collections. A simple creation but a lot of skill and experience was needed to make it; signed on the base with an H cane.

Harlequin Paperweight, Paul Ysart. Dia. 2.8", Height 2.1". $350/450. *Author's Collection.*

This is a good example of a Harlequin weight as it has many whole canes, including some extremely complex examples. From a side view, the cane ground is only one-eighth of an inch thick, and undulates in waves. The bubbles sit over depressions made by the steel pin that created the bubbles. The weight is signed on the sand-colored base with an H cane. I bought this piece at the 1992 Paul Ysart Exhibition of Paperweights, held at the Broadfield House Glass Museum, Kingswinford, England.

**Butterfly, Paul Ysart. Dia 2.8", Height 2".
$350/500.** *Courtesy of Terry and Hilary
Johnson.*

A pale blue-and-white butterfly hovers over a
jasper blue ground; simply made at an
affordable price. Signed with an H cane.

**Butterfly Paperweight, Paul Ysart. Dia. 2.8", Height
2". $600/800.** *Courtesy of Terry and Hilary Johnson.*

The wings of this butterfly are made entirely from
gold aventurine and makes this piece quite special.
The weight has a garland of spaced complex canes,
with one having the signature PY hidden within the
design. The insect hovers over a deep red ground,
with lengths of latticinio forming a crown.

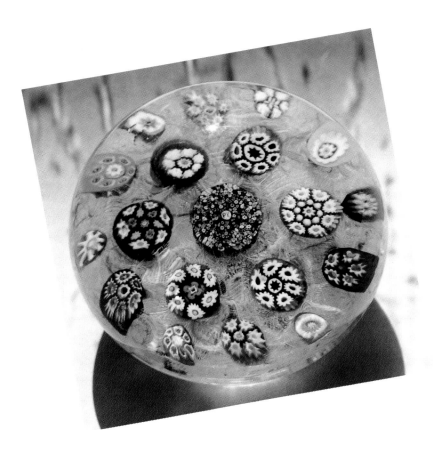

Spaced Concentric, Paul Ysart. Dia. 3", Height 2.8". $750/1000. *Courtesy of Terry and Hilary Johnson.*

Spiral twists of yellow and white canes make a bed for this nice selection of complex canes with one of Paul's special canes as a center point. This cane has a small PY sitting in the center of the cane, which has been constructed from no less than 200 individual cogs and tubes. All bundled together and stretched to a size where a strong loop is required to count the segments. This amazing cane can also be found in miniature paperweights with the cane segments on an even smaller scale.

Miniature Spaced Paperweight, Paul Ysart. Dia. 2.1", Height 1.5". $250/350. *Courtesy of Terry and Hilary Johnson.*

This miniature paperweight has a variety of complex canes set on a bright yellow ground with an H cane inserted in the base. The miniatures made at the Harland Glassworks came in a variety of colors but were usually spaced concentrics.

Hand written sale invoice.
Courtesy of Selkirk Glass.

The final sale invoice. *Courtesy of Selkirk Glass.*

These are the original and typed invoices for the sale of the Harland equipment when Paul Ysart finally retired from making paperweights. The equipment was sold to his friend Peter Holmes, who had established a glassworks with Ron Hutchinson to make paperweights in Selkirk. The sale of these items brought to a close the working career of Paul Ysart. The man and his work are sadly missed but neither will be forgotten.

PAUL YSART LIMITED

Harland, Reiss, Wick, Caithness KW1 7RR
Telephone: 0955-3317   Scotland

ITEM	PRICE
Kiln	£800
Marvers (2)	£ 8 each
Grinder	£100
Polisher	£ 80
Spare fan for Furnace	£ 50
Batch	£ 25
Vice	£ 5
Irons, iron tips, ladle welding rods, various rods.	£ 50
Small stand for glory hole.	£ 5
Screens (2)	£ 5 each
Total:-	£ 1141

Also included – Small quantity of fine clay, quite a few peersil bricks, including crown bricks, these items are included at no extra charge.

CHAPTER 12

JOHN DEACONS, "J" GLASS, CRIEFF GLASS AND ST KILDA, FOUNDED 1978

Crieff, Scotland

John Deacons decided to start his own glass house at the end of 1978 after learning his craft at Strathearn Glass in 1967, where he stayed for a year and then left with many of the other skilled paperweight makers to join Stuart Drysdale at the formation of Perthshire Paperweights. John stayed at Perthshire for over ten years. While there he perfected most of the skills required in paperweight making. John Deacons possessed the ambition and drive to branch out on his own and was in the fortunate position of having suitable buildings at the farm where he lived. He very quickly built his own pots and annealing ovens and started to make weights.

Initially he was on his own. Then he hired Allan Scott to help with the lampwork and aid him in producing enough to meet a rapidly filling order book. Most of their production was directed at the USA, in particular to a large department store in New York called Decora, and also to California, where the weights were distributed through Larry Selman Paperweights. All paperweights with a J cane were limited to a production of 100 pieces and one extra, which John kept as a reference piece. At this time, with production in full swing, two other names were used to identify production weights that did not go to the USA. These were signed with a StK cane for St Kilda and weights signed with a JD cane for John Deacons. All three signature canes and trading names were used during the life of J Glass. The majority of paperweights produced during this time were of exceptional quality.

The J Glass cane was inspired after a trip to a London auction house where John had seen a selection of antique Bohemian paperweights being sold, and signed with a lower case letter j and occasionally with a date of 1848. This j cane is thought to represent the Josephine Glassworks that was operational in the Bohemia/Silesia area in the early part of the 19th century. John was impressed by the quality and preciseness of these weights and set about emulating the old master glassmakers in artistic style and quality. John Deacons is a master craftsman who can produce almost any type of paperweight known with very little assistance. The weights produced during this period include single flowers and bouquets, butterflies, roses, crowns, Christmas editions, traditional millefiori and double overlays to an exacting standard.

In 1983, due to increasing competition and a slump in paperweight demand, John Deacons had to call in the receivers; he closed the business shortly after. He tried to revive the business as a going concern under the Crieff Glass label but survived for less than a year, after which John joined the unemployed list for nearly six months.

John Deacons is a man of great determination, so he set about restarting his career by building a small crib attached to his house, where he restarted his paperweight making on a very small scale. By 1985 he was selling weights directly to the public and retail gift shops. Due to his very low overheads, John was able to sell high quality paperweights at a price within everyone's reach. He covered a range of designs and styles that would have been out of reach for many collectors, including overlays and, incredibly, encased overlays. John perfected the encased overlay and made them in very small numbers. Collectors and dealers were quick to snap up these bargains.

John now has established a market share, and is slowly expanding at a regulated pace to meet new orders.

John Deacons making paperweights in his workshop. *Photo
Courtesy of Anne Metcalfe.*

**White Cherry Blossom Paperweight. Dia. 3.2", Height
2.1". $350/500.** *Author's Collection.*

Four open blossoms and four buds, attached to brown
stems with leaves, float midway in the brilliantly clear
crystal dome of this lovely weight. All paperweights are
signed. This weight has two rows of oval facets with a
large circular window on top. The base is hollow ground
to remove all trace of the pontil scar.

Vetch Wildflower Paperweight. Dia. 2.75", Height 1.7". $350/500. *Courtesy of Peter Hall.*

A lifelike representation of this once common grassland wildflower, which has now become a rare and protected species in England. This lampworked flower rests on a lacy bed of white latticinio. The weight has been faceted with six oval windows and a large top window. The base is precisely finished with all trace of the pontil ground out to a concave base.

Two Dragonflies and a Butterfly Paperweight. Dia. 3", Height 2.1". $500/600. *Author's Collection.*

The two dragonflies in this weight have wings made from white and colored spiral canes, which is a technique rarely used by Scottish makers and a welcome change to the elongated millefiori canes to be seen in the butterfly. This is an innovation that keeps John Deacons to the fore in paperweight design and production. This weight is signed with a J cane beneath the weight.

**Three Flower Paperweight. Dia. 3.3", Height 2.1".
$500/600.** *Author's Collection.*

The flower weights made during the early J Glass period
are of superb quality with most of the lampwork made
by Alan Scott. The realistic and stylized flowers have
petals that are slightly cupped to add a three-dimensional look, with sixteen side facets and a top window,
the spectator can view the interior from any position.
The weight is signed with a tiny cane of only one-
sixteenth of an inch diameter.

**J Glass Fantasy Flower Paperweight. Dia. 2.25",
Height 1.75". $250/350.** *Author's Collection.*

A stylized single flower with a stardust center. The
lilac and yellow flower has an outer layer of cupped
petals which gives the flower depth. The flower and
leaves are set against a dark ground, with the pontil
mark removed by grinding a concavity in the base.

**J Glass Concentric Paperweight. Dia. 3", Height 2.3".
$200/250.** *Author's Collection.*

Two rows of concentric millefiori canes fill out this
weight with the aid of the brick cut faceting. The base is
flat with a dark blue flashing to highlight the canes
formed into a letter V with the J cane signature beneath
the V.

**J Glass Butterfly Paperweight. Dia. 2.9", Height 2.25".
$200/300.** *Author's Collection.*

The wings of this butterfly are made from red and blue
canes with a J cane set in the right hand wing to
identify the maker. Set on a black ground with a ground
flat base. The insect has a green body with long yellow
antennae.

J Glass Dragonfly Paperweight. Dia. 3", Height 2.3". $200/300. *Courtesy of Pam and Roy Brown.*

Spiral latticinio cane has been used to create the wings of this dragonfly with a lilac body and black eyes. The weight has a J signature cane and a garland of red and white, and white stardust canes on the edge of the weight.

Flower Paperweight, St Kilda. Dia. 3", Height 2.25". $400/600. *Courtesy of Terry and Hilary Johnson.*

Three open yellow and lilac flowers with four buds set in clear glass make this paperweight a collector quality piece. It is signed with a quite rare StK cane and has five side windows and a top facet to view the insides. The lampwork during the J Glass period was made by Alan Scott, who has a very light and delicate touch when making flower petals and centers, as can be seen in this beautiful composition.

**Five Flower Paperweight, St. Kilda. Dia. 3",
Height 2.2". $400/600. *Courtesy of Terry and
Hilary Johnson.***

A double clematis type of flower with a further
three white and a single red flower makes a nice
arrangement on the black ground. The stamens in
the center of the flower heads are bunched tiny
black rods. Signed with a StK cane.

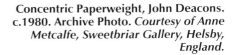

**Concentric Paperweight, John Deacons.
c.1980. Archive Photo. *Courtesy of Anne
Metcalfe, Sweetbriar Gallery, Helsby,
England.***

This is an early concentric from John Deacons
who had also worked at Perthshire Paperweights in Crieff, and in this example the style
of Perthshire can be seen. This weight is almost
a mirror image of many early Perthshire pieces,
the only difference is the Scottish thistle cane in
the center which was to become one of Johns
signature canes. This type of early weight can
still be found for around $75/100.

Intertwined Garland on Lace Paperweight, John Deacons. Dia. 2.9", Height 2.2". $100/150. *Author's Collection.*

This is a well made paperweight, with the millefiori canes all of the same size, and made in a steel mold to hold the canes firmly when being gathered up for the final addition of the glass dome. The set-up rests on a bed of white latticinio to compliment the brown and green canes. A hallmark of John Deacon's current work is the value for money weights he makes in a wide variety of styles and designs.

Crown and Pansy Paperweight, John Deacons. Dia. 2.7", Height 1.9". $150/200 *Author's Collection.*

A Pansy styled after an antique Baccarat, with a stardust cane center, rests on a bed of alternating colored rods formed in a crown. The canes are drawn beneath the weight to make a neat finish in the center. A white square tablet has a 1991 date in blue letters in the center of the base, and the JD signature cane can be seen on the top next to the Pansy stem.

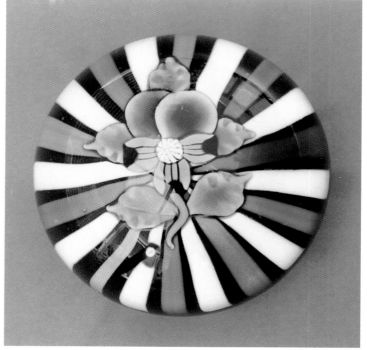

**Butterfly Paperweight, John Deacons. Dia. 2.7",
Height 1.9". $60/80. *Author's Collection.***

This weight was made around 1995 and has a JD
cane and a paper label with *"Made in Scotland by
John Deacons"* on the base. The weight has six side
facets and a top window. The design is set on a
black ground.

**Crown Hand Cooler, John Deacons. Archive
Photo. *Courtesy of Anne Metcalfe, Sweetbriar
Gallery, Helsby, England.***

Hand coolers were used in the 19th century by
ladies to stop hands perspiring and were quite
effective. This is a copy of a St Louis hand cooler
made around 1850 and would sell for around $75/
100, an original antique hand cooler would sell for
ten times this amount.

Basket of Flowers Paperweight, John Deacons. 1996. Dia. 3.75", Height 2.4". Archive Photo. *Courtesy of Anne Metcalfe, Sweetbriar Gallery, Helsby, England.*

This basket of flowers shows John's technical skill in creating a very difficult design. The flowers rest on a swirling bed of latticinio which forms the basket with a red and white torsade handle. The weight is then encased in a further gather of clear glass to finish off. This paperweight was sold at a very reasonable price in 1996 for $275.

Double Overlay Paperweights, John Deacons. Archive Photo. *Courtesy of Anne Metcalfe, Sweetbriar Gallery, Helsby, England.*

A fine selection of double overlay paperweights by John Deacons which have all been sold in 1997 to 1998 for $250 to 300. John is producing overlay paperweights at a price which makes them available to almost all collectors, and for only slightly more, he is encasing these double overlays in a final gather of clear glass.

Double Overlay Paperweights, John Deacons. Archive Photo. $250/300. *Courtesy of Anne Metcalfe, Sweetbriar Gallery, Helsby, England.*

This selection was again sold in 1997 to 1998 for an amazing price of $250 to $300. The weights all have well made flowers on a bed of latticinio and have all been faceted by Archie Anderson of Crieff, Scotland. The weights have the facets cut to a very high tolerance and are superbly finished and polished by Archie. This selection of double overlays is already changing hands for much more than the original prices.

CHAPTER 13

MACINTOSH GLASS, FALKIRK, SCOTLAND, 1981-87

Alistair MacIntosh trained at Edinburgh College of Art, which specializes in glass design. After learning glassmaking skills from two master glassmakers, he continued his education in the glass department of the College for a further five years. In 1979 he moved to Paisley College of Technology on a two year research project. He returned to his home town of Falkirk in 1987 to start his own business trading as MacIntosh Glass. This glass house made a wide variety of products which included paperweights, perfume bottles, vases and glassware.

The studio was particularly adept at a technique called *Vetro a Fili* (Glass of Threads) and most of his paperweights and perfume bottles incorporate this spiral glass design. The paperweights were rarely signed and then usually only if a piece had extra appeal, such as engraving. The items were all identified with a paper label which read MacIntosh, Falkirk. In the six years of trading, the company never incorporated any millefiori into their products, and about half the company output was sold to the retail gifts trade and the rest to corporate clients. The company was quite versatile and had even begun to make overlay glassware. The pontil marks were always removed from their work by grinding.

In 1987 Alistair closed his glassworks and joined the design team at Caithness Glass, where he is still employed.

Alistair MacIntosh trimming off waste glass, c. 1982.

"Fountain" Paperweights, MacIntosh.

These very simple paperweights were destined for the gifts trade, and were retailed around $15 each. This type of paperweight will rarely appreciate in value and although it was well made and functional, it has no artistic pretentions.

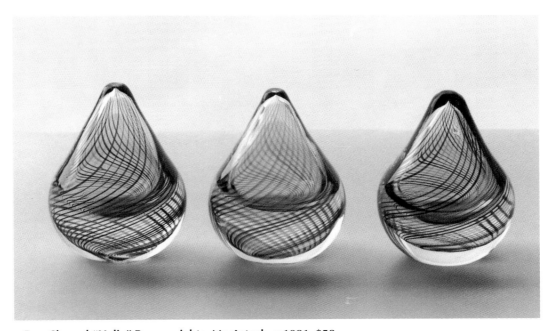

Pear Shaped "Helix" Paperweights, MacIntosh. c.1981. $50.

This type of weight has 32 colored rods inserted into a brass mold into which a gather of hot glass is lowered, to pick up the rods which adhere to the hot glass. The glassmaker then twists the glass, while still pliable, to impart the distinctive pattern. The paperweight is returned to the furnace for a final encasing of clear glass.

"Leny" Paperweight, MacIntosh. c.1987.

Various colors with tear drop bubbles inside make an ideal gift weight that sold in the stores for less than $15. They were an excellent value for the money and most collectors are gifted this type of weight at some point in their collecting careers.

Bubble Perfume Bottles and Paperweights, MacIntosh.

This range of inkwells, perfume bottles and paperweights were made in quite large numbers and can be found in several colors. No limited editions were ever made by this glassworks.

"Helix" Inkwell, Perfume Bottle and Paperweight, MacIntosh.

Once a design had been perfected the design would be incorporated into many other pieces, such as bowls, dishes and vases, and matching sets could be made up. The bowls and vases in this illustration are in a design known as "Rannoch."

Corporate Paperweight, Macintosh.

Paperweights made for corporate clients may number from a few dozen to several hundreds and many eventually find their way into antiques fairs and shops. This is an area of collecting that may eventually become a serious collectible side of the paperweight business. Nineteenth and early twentieth century advertising paperweights, usually with a paper photograph stuck to the base, are already being collected seriously in the USA and England with steadily rising values. Late Victorian weights of this type in good condition, fetch around $50/ 60, and anything relating to the Great Exhibition of 1851 in London can realize over $120.

Corporate Paperweight, MacIntosh.

This paperweight was made for the Scottish Development Agency as gifts for corporate visitors considering locating to Scotland. A well-made weight with a spiral interior design and a large window with the Scottish Agency Logo engraved on the face.

Paperweights and Inkwells, MacIntosh.

Colorful bubble inclusions in this selection make very decorative items in a modern home. These pieces are very skillfully made and designed.

CHAPTER 14

WILLIAM MANSON PAPERWEIGHTS, FOUNDED 1997

Perth, Scotland

William Manson, or Willie as he prefers to be known, has only recently started a business completely independent from any outside interference. "At last," he says, "I can design and develop paperweights to my satisfaction." This is a statement, from a man who had the privilege of being apprenticed to the 20th century's most gifted paperweight artist, Paul Ysart, and shows a determination to succeed where others have failed. He is reinforced in his conviction by his very supportive family, who all have a key role to play in this family business.

The business was founded only recently on a small industrial estate in Perth, Scotland, but Willie has a career in glassmaking that began with Caithness Glass in the late 1960s, under the guidance of Paul Ysart. When Paul left Caithness to establish the Harland Glassworks, he took Willie with him as his most gifted trainee. This relationship was to stand Willie in good stead all these years later, as he helped Paul to establish Harland Glass by preparing the small glassworks prior to production. Indeed it took the two men almost three months to equip the unit before a single weight was produced. At Harland, Willie quickly learned from the master, Paul Ysart, even to the making of their own canes. Willie stayed with Paul Ysart until the Harland business was dissolved in 1974, at which time he returned to Caithness as a fully skilled paperweight maker with considerable talent. One of Willie's specialities at which he is particularly adept he learned from Paul— the snake and salamander weight.

In 1979 Willie's skills were recognized by a company called Aden Hill Ltd, who recruited Willie from Caithness Glass to produce paperweights using Willie's name. They traded as William Manson Paperweights. The business flour-

ished for several years with three or four other employees helping Willie make weights. As well as quality collector paperweights that were always signed, another range, of a cheaper nature was produced to cater to the gifts trade. This range was unsigned and known as Scotia. In 1981, the business closed, unable to survive in the fierce business climate of the time.

Willie had no alternative but to return to Caithness Glass, who would always take back a worker with his skills. At this time he was also designing paperweights alongside his wife, Joyce, who also worked at Caithness. Husband and wife continued at Caithness designing and making paperweights in lampwork and traditional millefiori patterns until they took the plunge and opened up their own business.

The business has grown steadily with the help of the family and Willie's son William, who is already making weights that show much of his father's flair and skills. His daughter Carolyn is responsible for the office work and setting up of the lampworked designs prior to being encased in glass. The family are working together showing cohesive skills and adaptabily, which must ensure the future of this business in the long term.

Already Willie's weights are being exported to countries where they are eagerly collected by connoisseur collectors of glass and the general public alike. His strength appears to be in the enormous diversity and creativity of his designs, from simple flowers to snakes, frogs, teddy bears on the moon, pixies on mushrooms and all manner of traditional millefiori paperweights. Many of Willie's weights show the whimsy that his tutor Paul Ysart displayed in his later years. Paul's attention to detail and perfection is also clearly displayed in Willie's work. Manson paperweights can still be bought from around $100 to $400 and will surely appreciate as his fame and recognition spreads.

The Manson Family at work.

Working together in a studio on a small industrial estate in Perth, the family combines well with the task of running a profitable business in an area of intense competition. Trying to capture a percentage of a small but growing collector market is no mean feat in today's modern world. Carolyn is setting up the lampwork ready for the design to be collected by William who adds color before handing over to his father, to shape and finish off with the able assistance of Joyce.

A Lampwork Yellow Flower Set-Up. Willie Manson.

The lampwork design is created by Willie at the torch in small individual parts before being fused together.

Willie Manson examines the set-up.

Willie makes sure the set-up has not been distorted while being collected off the set-up plate, prior to the final encasing process.

Single Flower and Basket Paperweight, Willie Manson. Archive Photo. *Courtesy of Anne Metcalfe, Sweetbriar Gallery, Helsby, England.*

This weight was made in the early 1980s during Willie's Scotia days, and reflects the influence Paul Ysart had on his apprentices. The weight is testament to a skilled worker, trained by a master of the craft. Using skills honed to perfection under Paul Ysart, Willie has moved on to create work of the highest order in creativity and design, and now produces work to equal and even surpass his tutor.

Willie Manson Parrot Paperweight. Archive Photo. *Courtesy of Anne Metcalfe, Sweetbriar Gallery, Helsby, England.*

This Parrot weight was sold as a maker's sample in 1995 for $400 and again shows the Ysart influence on Willie. The parrot is extremely well constructed and life-like, and sits on a branch with leaves and a pink flower. The base of the paperweight has been flashed in a sky blue glass ground. The weight is signed with Willie's signature cane WM.

Upright Red Flower Paperweight, Willie Manson. Archive Photo. *Courtesy of Anne Metcalfe, Sweetbriar Gallery, Helsby, England.*

The star-cut base of this striking deep red flower composition, made during Willie's Caithness days, gives the weight added interest in this maker's one-off example. Sold for a bargain price in 1998 of $330.

Snake Paperweight, Willie Manson. Dia. 3", Height 2.2". $350/500. *Author's Collection.*

This snake weight is in a limited edition of 150, and made in 1993 while Willie worked for Caithness Glass. The design of the snake body is first made in lampworked green aventurine and the yellow markings on the body are made by trailing tiny amounts of hot glass on to the body, before the final dome of glass is added. Signed with a WM cane.

Mice Paperweight, Willie Manson. Dia. 3", Height 2.1". $250/400. *Author's Collection.*

An unsigned paperweight made by Willie during his Scotia days around 1980. The three mice sit on a sand and rocky ground with a base flashed in dark red that is perfectly flat. This may have been an early piece as the mouse tails are a little untidy and long.

Lizard Paperweight, Willie Manson.1998. $450/500. *Courtesy of Dave and Susan Brett, Select Paperweights, London.*

Paperweights made by Willie in his new venture are taking his artistic talent to the limit. His new designs incorporate textured glass on the outside, with a large facet cut to reveal a lizard in a cave with flowers on a mottled ground. This lizard is made in a limited edition of 25.

Double Lizard Paperweight, Willie Manson. c.1993. Archive Photo. *Courtesy of Anne Metcalfe, Sweetbriar Gallery, Helsby, England.*

Multi-faceted with a large top window, this double Lizard weight was sold for $450 in 1997 and would be a welcome addition to anyone's collection.

Blue Flashed Puffin Paperweight, Willie Manson. $250/300. *Author's Collection.*

This weight was made in a limited edition of 100 during Willie's Caithness days, and has Caithness etched on the base with edition size.

Snowman Paperweight, Willie Manson. c.1994. Archive Photo. *Courtesy of Anne Metcalfe, Sweetbriar Gallery, Helsby, England.*

A Christmas weight made at Caithness and sold for approximately $350. The weight has pure white snow on a blue flashed ground, with a colorful snowman and a fir tree. Five side facets with a large top window through which a happy snowman can be seen.

**Red Breasted Sticklebacks in a Jam Jar, Willie Manson.
Height 3.5", $450,** *Courtesy of Anne Metcalfe,
Sweetbriar Gallery" Helsby, England.*

This is quite a novel way of displaying fish and takes you back to pre-teen days down by the stream with a long cane and net on the end. This weight should prove popular with all fishermen. This weight was made in 1996, but Willie still makes these on request.

Toadstool and Flower Paperweight, Willie Manson. $450. *Courtesy of Dave and Susan Brett, Select Paperweights, London.*

This newly made upright weight has a textured rough finish to the back of the weight which sits on a flat cut base. The weight is signed with a WM cane.

Collaborative Paperweight, Willie and William Manson. $550/650. *Courtesy of Dave and Susan Brett, Select Paperweights, London.*

This paperweight was made by son, William Jr., with a little help from his father who made the lovely Butterfly for him. The other lampwork was made by the son and already shows tremendous skill for a young man still learning the trade. With such a talented father, we should be seeing wonderful creations in the near future. This weight has the added attraction of being a double overlay, with the whole weight faceted by Archie Anderson who does all the faceting for the Mansons and John Deacons. This weight is signed and has a star cut base.

Double Overlay Yellow Flower Paperweight, William Manson. $550/650. *Courtesy of Dave and Susan Brett, Select Paperweights, London.*

This is another example of this young man's skill, with all the different processes involved accomplished by himself. An unusual feature of the base is a lattice work cut. The weight is signed with a WM cane, but William shortly will be using his own signature cane as he has the same initials as his father.

Profile of William Manson Double Overlay Paperweight.

Fish Paperweight, Willie Manson. 1998. $100/150.
Courtesy of Dave and Susan Brett, Select Paper-
weights, London.

The Manson family are now producing a range of
excellent quality paperweights but at a budget price.
These weights are full size and have a range of
subjects that will encourage new and established
collectors to add Manson weights to their collections.

Flower Paperweight, Willie Manson. 1998. $100/
150. *Courtesy of Dave and Susan Brett, Select*
Paperweights, London.

A simple yellow flower with bud and leaves, signed
with a WM cane set in crystal clear glass will surely
make these budget weights a winning combination
for the Mansons.

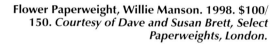

Fish Paperweight, Willie Manson. 1998. $100/150.
Courtesy of Dave and Susan Brett, Select Paperweights,
London.

This fish weight represents excellent value for money for
the detail that is included in this piece. With two fish,
rocks, anemones and a textured finish, the weight also
has a WM cane to add value to a good gift weight.

Swan Paperweight, Willie Manson. 1998. $100/ 150. *Courtesy of Dave and Susan Brett, Select Paperweights, London.*

A delightful paperweight with two flower heads made in the Paul Ysart style, very simple but very effective against a dark blue background and a well constructed white swan on a pond. Signed with a WM cane.

Paperweights and Packaging, Willie Manson. 1998.

Paperweights dispatched by the Mansons arrive safely in these neat wooden packing cases. Each weight is packed individually to ensure the paperweight arrives in the same condition as it leaves the studio.

CHAPTER 15

FAKES, COPIES AND REPRODUCTIONS

It could be said that any copy or duplicate paperweight is praise for the original artist, but if the item is reproduced to snare the unwary and uninformed with a profit motive, then the practice is despicable. The word copy is often used to describe something that is not as good as the original, but in some of the following examples, which have been labeled as copies, this is not so.

As yet the makers of these weights have not been identified, despite considerable speculation, and the only signature canes to be found in these paperweights is a PY cane for Paul Ysart, and a J cane purporting to be by John Deacons, made during his Jay glass years. Paperweights with a PY cane in these so called copies have been labeled as fakes because of a slipped Y, the Y appears to be set a little lower than the P. But it may well be that Paul Ysart made the cane with the slipped Y, and that the construction of the signature cane shows a slight aberration from the normal and nothing more sinister than that. Examples of slipped letters and variations in signature canes can be found throughout the recent book *The Dictionary of Paperweight Signature Canes* by Andrew H.Dohan, published by Paperweight Press. This book shows examples of all the paperweight makers' signature canes and where a maker has pulled many rods during his career, the signature cane can show tremendous variation in color, shape and size, with nothing unusual in a slipped digit or letter. However paperweights with a slipped cane may be subject to suspicion because Paul Ysart himself knew that his own canes had been *"misappropriated, and have been used in paperweights made by other glassworkers."* It is a pity that Paul Ysart wasn't asked about this suspected signature cane.

The first two pieces illustrated with PY canes are of a good standard and worthy of a Paul Ysart attribution, but when these fakes appeared on the market in volume in the late 1980s they caused confusion and alarm, and in one particular case severe financial hardship. What was thought to be a suspicious feature in this saga was the amount of paperweights to come onto the collecting market in one lot. These weights were sold through dealers and auction houses in Scotland and England, and were offered in batches of fifteen or twenty with the slipped PY cane. The unsuspecting dealers were duped into selling these weights with a du-

bious history to an eager collecting public, until alarm bells began to ring when the quality of some of these weights was called into question. When collectors found out that their Ysart weights may not be Paul Ysart's work after all, many demanded their money back from their supplier. One dealer is still sitting on a stock of suspect paperweights that cannot be sold as genuine Paul Ysart paperweights because of continuing suspicions.

The volume of paperweights entering the market should have rung alarm bells, but large volumes of Paul's work have at times been released on to the market by Paul himself and others connected to him. As an example, Bert Gunn, Paul Ysart's business partner in the Harland Glassworks, released over 150 genuine paperweights that had been in storage for nearly 15 years for an exhibition of Paul Ysart Paperweights held at The Broadfield House Glass Museum, England; most of these were offered for sale after the exhibition. During 1997–1998, in order to take advantage of rising prices in Paul's paperweights, Bert Gunn released to dealers the remainder of his stock of paperweights that had been made by Paul Ysart during his Harland years. Many of the supposedly inferior signed weights may reflect early and experimental pieces made by Paul. When Bert Gunn released his last batch of weights, many were not of the highest quality and some had slight flaws and distorted canes. These weights were the last that he possessed, and had been picked over by dealers. Could this also apply to the better quality and signed PY weights that are supposed to be fakes? One does not know.

Many of these weights have Vasart canes included within the designs, and can be very well made. It is now recognized that canes survive the glassworks that made them. Whenever I see any of these suspect paperweights being offered for sale, it is usually through the same outlets, and when asked about the weights and their history they are never described as by Paul Ysart, even though there may be a PY cane within, and no opinion is offered as to attribution, and the usual response is that *"you probably know more about paperweights than I do, you decide."* Paul Ysart paperweights with a slipped Y cane have also been found in American paperweight collections, so this is not just a British problem. The situation probably arose because English dealers were selling to American collectors, who were at the time in complete ignorance of the suspected fakes. It was not until members of the Cambridge Paperweight Circle became suspicious of the large volume appearing on the market that alarm bells were rung, and credit must be given to the members who drew attention to the suspected fakes and canes used. Many of these paperweights are obvious copies, but for some you will have to decide on the authenticity for yourself.

Patterned Millefiori Paperweight, Paul Ysart. Dia. 3", Height 2".
Author's Collection.

This is a well documented fake paperweight with a Paul Ysart signature cane. The central feature cane is a known Vasart cane that can also be found in an inkwell in the Vasart chapter. The rest of the canes are well made and neatly arranged in a square pattern, enclosing lengths of colored spiral cane. As Paul Ysart made many different sized weights, with many variations of base finish, I do not think size or base finish could provide conclusive proof of fake or the genuine article alone, but the selection I have seen, when compiling this chapter, have all had the pontil removed by grinding, which may or may not be significant.

Base of Previous Paperweight.

The PY cane can be seen clearly with a slight slipping of the Y in relation to the P. I would be surprised if Paul had abandoned the cane to the scrap bin, even if he noticed that the letters were not quite correctly aligned. I suspect he would have continued to use the cane, which clearly shows his initials?

Garlanded Flower Paperweight, Paul Ysart. Dia. 3", Height 2".
Author's Collection.

A striking red flower weight with a very complex center cane, made up of 20 separate components. Set on a black ground and garlanded with a row of millefiori canes that can be found in other fakes. A high degree of skill has gone into the making of this nice weight, and I am sure that if Paul Ysart did not make it, then whoever did must surely be one of the more skillful makers in the paperweight making fraternity today. The base is ground to a slight concavity to remove the pontil mark.

Three Row Concentric signed PY. Dia. 3.1", Height 2".
Courtesy of Terry and Hilary Johnson.

A slightly squashed PY cane sits between the two outside rows of typical Paul Ysart style canes. The light brown and orange canes around the central complex canes look a little odd, which could arouse suspicion. At an English auction, I would have expected this weight with a Paul Ysart attribution, to fetch around $600/700. As a fake the price could be almost as much, because these pieces have as much interest as the genuine article, if not more.

Butterfly Paperweight. Dia. 3.2", Height 2".
Courtesy of Terry and Hilary Johnson.

A well made butterfly in the Paul Ysart style, that hovers over a pale blue ground with speckles of dust and sand showing, which may be intentional or not. If this was a test or an experimental piece it was too good to scrap because of a faulty ground. Signed with a PY cane with a slipped Y. The butterfly is precisely made and a good example to compare with known Ysart weights.

A close-up of the PY cane with a slipped Y. *Courtesy of Roy and Pam Brown.*

The close-up shows the Y slightly below the P and is thought to be a distinguishing feature in fake paperweights.

Close-up of genuine Paul Ysart Signature Cane. *Courtesy of Roy and Pam Brown.*

The signature cane can be seen in the center of the blue flower.

As far as I know, a paperweight with a slipped Y has never been offered for sale at auction labeled as a fake. This makes this piece extremely hard to value. A weight such as this would I am sure command a respectable price for its construction and historical significance, and is a very attractive paperweight despite its uncertain provenance. A price of $200 plus would seem to be in order but I would not be surprised to see it realize a lot more. The paperweight is well made on a crown of green and white latticinio rods with the flower heads just being a little too heavily made to make it of Paul Ysart quality.

Four Flower Posy. Dia. 3.25", Height 2.3". $200+.
Author's Collection.

This weight was bought in August 1998 at Newark Showground, England, from a dealer who had this paperweight on display with one other signed PY weight of similar quality. This paperweight comes complete with two small bruises for authenticity. If these weights are ever proved to be early Paul Ysarts, then I shall have my regret but until they are I shall buy no more, unless the demand and price for fake weights goes up. Nicely made with a typical bow of ribbon around the posy Paul Ysart style, but with heavy flower heads to let the weight down a little.

Four Leaf Clover with Garland. Dia. 2.9", Height 2".
Courtesy of Roy and Pam Brown.

Paul Ysart did make clover-leaf weights during his years at Moncrieff's and remembered the design well, but when he was shown a photograph of this weight, he stated that he *"definitely did not make it."* Set on a mottled ground with a garland of simple canes, the stalk is slightly detached from the leaves, something that Paul Ysart would be careful to avoid.

**Posy and Aventurine Striped Flower. Dia. 3",
Height 2.3".** *Courtesy of Roy and Pam Brown.*

An attractive set-up of flowers and leaves, with a large blue clematis type flower as a center piece with striped aventurine petals. The PY cane is set within a small flower head, the same as Paul discreetly placed his signature cane, but the flower heads are rather clumsily made, when compared to a genuine Ysart flower.

Moth with Millefiori Garland. Dia. 2.9", Height 2.1". *Courtesy of Roy and Pam Brown.*

This would have been a rare piece if genuine, as a moth has never been attributed to Paul Ysart. The moth is identified by the absence of antenna on the head, large eyes and thick triangular body. The insect flies over a mottled green ground with a garland of complex millefiori canes in red and lilac. Paul Ysart was shown a photograph of this moth and denied ever having made it, even though it is signed with a PY cane.

Two Flower Paperweight. Dia. 3.2", Height 2.3". *Courtesy of Terry and Hilary Johnson.*

Of all the suspected fake paperweights illustrated so far, this and the next two are by far the most suspect. The lampworked flowers are extremely ham-handed in comparison to the delicate flowers made by Paul Ysart. These efforts would not fool the majority of collectors today but did ensnare new, and even the knowledgable collectors before it was realized these pieces were, in fact, copies. This was the case when these weights were purchased from a single Scottish source in the early 1990s, before it was realized that fakes were being made in considerable quantities. When these paperweights are seen alone, they could easily pass for early, or prototype, paperweights, made as part of the learning curve that all artists have to make before becoming proficient in their chosen art form. As they are all signed with a PY cane any clumsiness about the weight would have been discounted. It is only when placed alongside the genuine article that the differences can be seen. The flower heads are little more than lumps of colored glass with little or no finesse. The only quality part of the weight is in fact the actual PY signature cane, which is clear and does not have a slipped Y and may be another version of a fake PY cane, or could even be an original cane from Paul Ysart's "misappropriated" cane stock.

Single Clematis Flower with Small Flower heads. Dia. 3.2", Height 2.3". *Courtesy of Terry and Hilary Johnson.*

Set on a bubbly orange ground with a well made PY cane next to the thick stem. The paperweight does not have the delicate touch associated with Paul Ysart's better work. A petal has slipped in the encasing process to spoil the weight even further.

Double Clematis Flower. Dia. 3.2". Height 2.3". *Courtesy of Terry and Hilary Johnson.*

A good central complex millefiori cane adds interest to this rather clumsy and heavy piece, it may have been made at the start of this particular maker's career in the art of deception. Made on the same orange background as the previous paperweight with the pontil lightly ground out.

Genuine and Suspect Paul Ysart Paperweights. *Courtesy of Roy and Pam Brown.*

When seen together the suspect paperweight on the right does tend to look a little clumsy in comparison to its neighbor, which is finer in construction, and has a delicate and artistic touch to the clematis petals in the central flower. Both are signed with a PY cane and the signature in the weight on the right has the slipped Y cane. On close examination, the suspect signature cane has been slightly distorted in the making, which may account for the digits not being square to each other.

Close-Up of PY Cane.

The Y looks slightly lower than the P in this signature cane, but may just be a small variance in the cane pulling process. The main reason for this signature cane being suspect is that it is commonly found in this type of slightly inferior paperweight.

Genuine PY Signature Cane. *Courtesy of Roy and Pam Brown.*

In this example, the signature cane is hidden in a millefiori cane but in most cases the PY cane is easily found, and is much larger than this tiny specimen.

Close Packed Millefiori Paperweight. Anonymous Artist. $150/200. Dia. 3", Height 2". *Courtesy of Terry and Hilary Johnson.*

Very colorful canes are scrambled together to make this a bright and cheerful paperweight. Originating in Scotland, this piece has several known Vasart canes, including the blue and white striped cane on the right hand side, which can be found also in the following inkwell and in a Vasart inkwell in the chapter on Vasart. A lot of time and trouble would have gone into the making of these very varied and complex canes.

Millefiori Inkwell. Dia. 3.5" Height 4.5", $150/200.
Courtesy of Terry and Hilary Johnson.

Spaced canes divided by colored spirals in clear glass make for an attractive desk ornament and paperweight. Unsigned but with a sprinkling of Vasart canes including the blue and white cane in the stopper. An attractive piece and well worth the $150 or so it cost.

Millefiori Green Inkwell. Dia. 3.5", Height 4.5".
Unknown Maker. $200/250.
Author's Collection.

At first sight I thought I had discovered a very nice example of a Vasart inkwell with several recognizable canes within. But on closer examination it proved to be a reproduction. I was fooled by the coloring and spiral effect around the neck of the bottle. The coloring of the canes are much stronger than in genuine Vasart inkwells, and the stoppers in Vasart pieces in my own collection measure only 1.3" in diameter whereas in this and other similar examples the stopper is much larger at 1.8", a significant size difference. The construction and cane placement is almost identical in both pieces, but the price of original Vasart inkwells bares no relation to these reproductions, and recently a good example of a genuine Vasart inkwell realized $1300 in an American auction in 1998.

Spaced with Garland of Complex Canes. Dia. 3", Height 2". Unknown Maker. $120/150. *Courtesy of Terry and Hilary Johnson.*

This paperweight originates from the same Scottish source as the inkwells. A very nice weight with brightly colored canes set on a green ground with segments of canes set into a pure white casing. This white cane can be found in many examples from this source of inkwells and paperweights.

Close Packed Inkwell. Dia. 3.5", Height 4.5". Unknown Maker. $150/200. *Author's Collection.*

Dozens of bright complex canes pack this piece to overflowing and it is a good reference piece for identifying weights from this maker. The base has been flashed in red with the pontil left unground.

Close Packed Inkwell. Dia. 3", Height 5.5". Unknown Maker. $120/150. *Author's Collection.*

A slight variation to the normal inkwell, this one has a distinctive button where the canes have been collected from the holding plate, and has no lip or rim; very similar to some old English pieces that are usually described as "ladies' inkwells or scent bottles." Packed with very complex canes in all colors and styles.

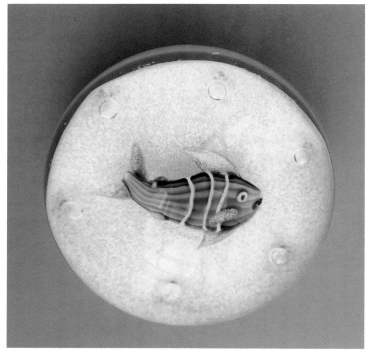

Fish Paperweight, Paul Ysart. Dia. 2.9", Height 2.1". $250/300. *Author's Collection.*

This fish weight could be regarded as suspect because it does not have any signature cane or sticker attached. However this weight was made by Paul at the Harland works, and does not include an H cane with which he signed all his fish weights made at this period in his career. The fish has untidy stripes and a tail end that has not been finished very well, looking as though the end has broken off. The sand-colored ground is so thinly applied that where the glass was pierced to make the bubbles it is possible to see through the ground. The dome has several small pieces of detritus floating around and in several places the sides show a roughness that has been missed in the final polishing. All in all not one of Paul's best, but an example of a genuine Paul Ysart weight, purchased from his ex-business partner in the Harland venture. It could be interpreted as a fake because of poor quality. Every glassmaker produces paperweights that are not always of a standard that they would like but these weights are put to one side, as this weight was. Too good to put in the scrap bin but not for immediate sale and the last piece to be chosen by dealer or collector.

In Conclusion

It is a fact that paperweights have been produced by one or two makers using "misappropriated" signature and other millefiore canes made by Paul Ysart. Some of these fake Ysart weights are of such poor construction that they become obvious when placed next to genuine weights, even if they do contain a PY cane, but it is when these weights are seen alone that the unwary may be tempted into parting with their money. So the message is, do not buy a suspect weight of dubious quality, do not be tempted by a PY cane if the workmanship of the whole piece is not of the highest quality that is always associated with Paul Ysart's paperweights, unless the source of the paperweight can be guaranteed, as with the previous weight bought from Bert Gunn.

BIBLIOGRAPHY

Jokelson, Paul. *Sulphides,* Galahad Books, New York City.

Andrews, Frank. *Ysart Glass.* Volo Edition Ltd, Ferme Park Road, London.

Dohan, Andrew H. *Paperweight Signature Canes.* Paperweight Press, 123 Locust Street, Santa Cruz, USA.

GLOSSARY

Annealing. All paperweights and glass articles must be cooled very slowly, the time depending on the mass of the article concerned. A paperweight would be left in a slowly cooling oven for approximately 24 hours. This slow cooling process prevents cracking of the glass.

Air Bubbles. Silvery air bubbles can be added to the inside of a paperweight, as seen in a dump weight, by piercing the still soft glass with a sharp steel pin or steel comb. This traps a small amount of air inside, and when the pin is withdrawn, closing the hole, the trapped air will expand on reheating the glass.

Baccarat. French Glasshouse. Perhaps the most famous of paperweight makers in the 19th century, and still producing quality paperweights and millefiori objects today.

Basal Ring. This refers to that part of the paperweight base, which touches the surface that the paperweight is resting on. When a paperweight has its pontil mark removed by grinding, a shallow depression is formed which usually extends outwards towards the edge, leaving a flat area of approximately 0.25 inch to rest upon. This prevents scratching and obscuring the canework beneath the paperweight.

Basket. A basket describes the outer row of canes drawn down and beneath the paperweight, enclosing the bottom half of the weight.

Batch. After the sand and other ingredients are melted down in the furnace, the glass becomes known and referred to as "the batch."

Billet. A lump or slug of clear glass.

Bohemia. An area, which includes Czechoslovakia and much of Eastern Europe, that produced glassware and paperweights in the classic period.

Button. "On the button" is a term used to describe the set-up of canes after they have been removed from the steel or iron mold. Not being much bigger than a button, the magnifying property of the glass dome on a paperweight enlarges the button to make it fill out the weight.

Canes. The basic element in the majority of concentric paperweights. Pliable glass of a single color is drawn out by two glassworkers attaching a pontil rod on either end of a lump of glass approximately three inches in diameter and six inches long. The workers will then move away from each other holding the glass three feet above the floor, as the glass is pulled in two directions the center reduces down to approximately 0.25 inch and cools. The cane continues to be drawn out to forty or fifty feet in length. After thirty seconds to allow cooling, the rod is laid on the floor and cut into one foot lengths with pincers.

Carpet Ground. This description applies when the same canes are used to cover the bottom element of the paperweight, usually other more colorful canes will then be set into this "carpet."

Classic Period. Any paperweights described as from "the classic period" means they were made around 1845 to 1852. This was the height of the English and French paperweight popularity, when most of the quality pieces were made.

Clichy, French Glasshouse. A major producer of superior quality paperweights in the 19th century.

Close Packed. Canes bundled together and held in no particular order or pattern before being encased in the final covering of glass.

Cog Cane. This can be a simple one color rod, formed in a serrated mold, and may be the base for a more complex cane.

Complex Cane. This is a combination of many smaller rods and canes, as many as one hundred bundled together, reheated and drawn out to miniaturize the cane to normal size. A magnifying glass is then required to appreciate its complexity.

Concentric. The majority of English paperweights were "concentrics." From a central large cane, rings of ever increasing circles of millefiori canes reach out to the edge of the weight. Usually five or six rows, but as many as eight rows have been found.

Crib. A crib is a word used to describe a small glassworks, usually at the glassmaker's home and worked by one or two people.

Cushion. The canes are set in rings of metal before being picked up by the soft glass on the end of a pontil rod. This gives the appearance of a pin cushion.

Dipping. This was a method of covering and adding a further amount of colored glass to overlay a paperweight. The weight was dipped into the required color to pick up just sufficient to cover the top, this added glass was then pulled and pushed all over the object with the worker's pliers and tweezer type tools, to create a thin layer of a different color. The object is then reheated and smoothed off. Further coats can then be added.

Facet. Many weights were cut on the sides and top to allow the viewer an unobstructed view of the internal motif. This could be a flat or concave cut of approximately 1 inch.

Flash. This is a thin layer of colored glass sometimes applied all over, or just to the base of a weight. If applied all over, windows are normally cut to allow viewing inside the weight, as with an overlay weight.

Foot. Paperweights and inkwells have this feature to break up the outline. The foot is created by applied pressure with a pair of steel tongs while the glass is still soft.

Frigger. Friggers are pieces of work made by the glassworkers with and without the knowledge of the management. The purpose could be to use up waste glass, expand on skills and new techniques, or for use as gifts for family and friends.

Gather. A gather of glass is a lump of molten glass, taken from the furnace, to form another part of the paperweight, such as the dome.

Glory Hole. This refers to the entrance opening of the glass furnace where paperweights can be reheated to a working temperature.

Latticinio or Lace. Normal diameter rods with spiral twists of white or colored threads, with the length being longer than the diameter, sometimes used as a base on which other millefiori canes are set.

Lampwork. This is the method used to create flowers and other worked items, using a small torch with a gas and oxygen mixture and a small, fine hot flame. Glass can be worked into any shape imaginable.

Magnum. This refers to the size given to a paperweight that is of a larger diameter than normal, usually over 3.75 inches.

Marver Plate. This is a solid steel plate used by the glassworkers to roll out and shape the soft glass. It is on this plate that the glass can become contaminated with dust and dirt, and although not seen while the glass is in this semi-molten stage, particles of dirt show up in a magnified version when the paperweight is cold.

Millefiori. Originating in Italy, millefiori means a thousand flowers, as most millefiori canes are said to look like flower heads. Millefiori canes hve been used in glass from the 2nd century A.D.

Overlay. The paperweight has further colored glass added to encase the outside of the weight, which can then be cut with windows, to allow the insides to be seen.

Pontil Rod and Mark. This is a steel rod that can be hollow to allow air to be blown through, in order to expand the glass in size, and to gather the glass from the furnace. The paperweight is formed and worked while attached to this rod. When the weight is ready to be detached from the pontil rod, air is gently blown on the stem of glass attached to the paperweight, this cooling allows the glassworker to tap the rod sharply, allowing the finished paperweight to fall into a soft flame resistant material, after which it is taken immediately to the annealing oven. When cool and annealed the rough mark where the weight was attached to the rod is removed by grinding. Many glass houses never removed this mark if it did not protrude below the base of the weight.

Pastry Mold Cane. This cane is usually deeply serrated with the bottom being flared out larger than the top, as with a lady's skirt.

Ridge Mark. When the cane set-up is picked up from the steel or iron mold, by a gather of glass, the two halves stick together and usually leave an indentation where the two halves meet. This is quite common on English paperweights.

Set-ups. This describes the millefiori canes that have been cut to the desired lengths, usually about 0.25 of an inch, which are then sorted into size and design, and with the help of tweezers placed into a steel or iron ring mold with a base. The designs are set in concentric circles, starting from the outside edge, and with ever decreasing circles towards the center where usually a much larger cane will be used to centralise the set-up.

Silhouette Cane. Heads and animals are the usual subjects in these canes that are viewed in cross section after molding, and being drawn out and cut.

Spaced Millefiori. Where canes are placed in the paperweight in a nongeometric pattern but with spaces between them.

Saint Louis. A notable French Glasshouse which produced paperweights and related glassware in the classic period, especially fine concentrics.

Striae. This word is used to describe the stress lines that can sometimes be seen in glass paperweights.

The almost transparent lines are caused by the near molten glass being twisted and turned in the working process. Occasionally these lines are on the surface caused by pressure on the dome by the tools used to smooth and shape the final gather of glass. The lines can be felt with the tips of the fingers if on the surface, like slight ripples, and can cause distortion to the motif inside the weight. However, they can be polished out if on the surface, but nothing can be done with internal lines.

Sulphide. A molded ceramic glass paste portrait of a famous person which is then encased in a gather of glass to form a paperweight, or for decorating other objects.

Torsade. A twisted cane that normally encircles the bottom of a paperweight like a rope.

More Schiffer Titles

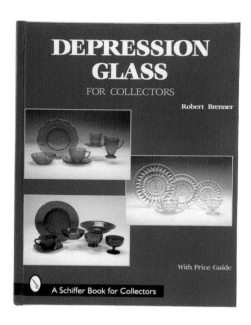

Depression Glass for Collectors Robert Brenner. Recently hailed as one of the top collectibles sought on the Internet, Depression Glass has attracted the interest of many young enthusiasts. From Adam to Windsor, readers of this book will soon become familiar with these pattern names as well as gain a richer appreciation of this tableware's history and its value today. Very inexpensive when first produced, Depression Glassware was America's early experimentation with the mold-etched method for producing pattern glass. Today collectors recognize the beauty and creativity of the glass artisans during this period. Whether a beginning or a veteran collector, some very exciting discoveries await the reader as the pages are turned. Hundreds of glass pieces photographed in full color are accompanied by a price guide to help the collector determine the current value for these colorful and elegant pieces. Anyone who has ever found a piece of Depression glass in a relative's house, seen pieces at an antique show, or been attracted by its design and color, will find this book fascinating.

Size: 8 1/2" x 11"	343 color photos	176 pp.
Price Guide		
ISBN: 0-7643-0670-7	hard cover	$24.95

Depression Era: Art Deco Glass Leslie Piña & Paula Ockner. From Anchor Hocking's Manhattan pattern to Carder and Teague designs for Steuben, all of the major American companies who made Art Deco glass during the Depression Era—Cambridge, Consolidated, Duncan, Fostoria, Heisey, Libbey, Morgantown, Tiffin, and many others—are presented in this long-awaited book. With more than 350 color photos of both popular and rare examples, informative captions with values, plus patent drawings, company information, a bibliography, and a detailed index, this book will delight anyone interested in this highly collectible American glassware or in the Art Deco style.

Size: 8 1/2" x 11"	350 color photos	160 pp.
Price Guide		Index
ISBN: 0-7643-0718-5	hard cover	$24.95

Depression Era Stems & Tableware: Tiffin Ed Goshe, Ruth Hemminger & Leslie Piña. This book represents an extraordinary sample of Depression era glass, because Tiffin was an extraordinary glass company. Its output during the Depression was well documented and enough to keep any collector occupied for years. Most of the glass presented in this volume is from the 1920s and 1930s. With detailed captions for the more than 450 illustrations--color photographs, catalog pages, advertisements, and drawings--it is a guide to help the collector, researcher, and dealer identify, price, and enjoy this compelling glassware.

Size: 11" x 8 1/2"	450 illustrations	176 pp.
Price Guide Index		
ISBN: 0-7643-0652-9	hard cover	$29.95

Frederick Carder and Steuben Glass: American Classics Thomas P. Dimitroff, Charles R. Hajdamach, Jane Shadel Spillman, and Robert F. Rockwell III. This essential reference work provides a detailed study of Frederick Carder, his contributions to the Steuben Glass Works, and the captivating works of art he produced in glass. To dazzle and delight the reader, there are over 760 photographs and 450 line drawings, the vast majority of which provide illustration for 800 pieces of Steuben glass from the famous Rockwell collections. Reference material and photographs never before in print are provided. The text evaluates Carder and the Steuben Glass Works that he cofounded in 1903 in a critical light. It reviews Carder's lengthy and productive career, analyzes his changing role within the company, and places Carder's artistic contributions within the matrix of the international decorative arts industries of his time. A section valuable to all collectors is one in which many aspects of identification and evaluation are covered--signatures, relative rarity, and dating.

Size: 9" x 12" 495 color photos, 720 b/w images 400 pp.
Price Guide
ISBN: 0-7643-0486-0 hard cover $125.00

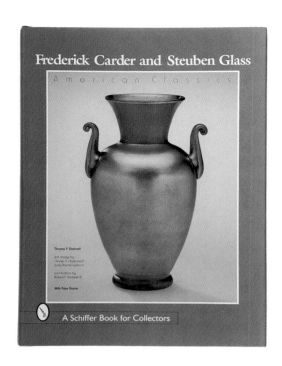

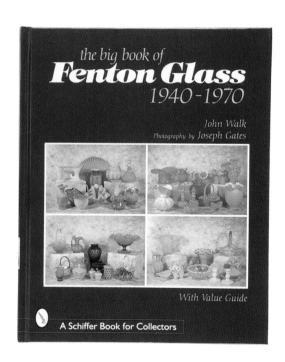

The Big Book of Fenton Glass:1940-1970 John Walk with photography by Joseph Gates. This is a beautiful and comprehensive guide to the glassware produced by the Fenton Art Glass Company from the 1940s through the 1960s. The various colors, decorative treatments, and forms (from baskets and bowls to sandwich trays and vases) are vividly displayed in over 840 color photographs. A large selection of rare, unlisted, and experimental items--some never before pictured--are included. In the text, a brief history of the company is provided. Additional information provides listings of factory ware and mold numbers along with a chronicle of the various colors produced in the many product lines. Also included in the book are a bibliography and values for the glassware in its many eye-catching forms and brilliant colors.

Size: 9" x 12" 844 color photos 208 pp.
Price Guide
ISBN: 0-7643-0582-4 hard cover $29.95

Morgantown Glass: From Depression Glass Through the 1960s Jeffrey B. Snyder. This beautiful glassware, produced in Morgantown, West Virginia, is displayed in over 860 color photographs. The decorations that adorn this brilliant glassware are illustrated among the photographs. The reader will become familiar with the striking colors, etchings, cuttings, and cased filament stems used to make Morgantown glass distinctive and immediately appealing. Included in the text are a history of the Morgantown Glass Works (under various names and ownerships), a review of glass making techniques--including descriptions of specific techniques given by Morgantown employees themselves, and a survey of the decorative techniques employed by the firm. A detailed bibliography, an index, and values round out the presentation.

Size: 8 1/2" x 11" 860+ color photos 224 pp.
Price Guide
ISBN: 0-7643-0504-2 hard cover $29.95

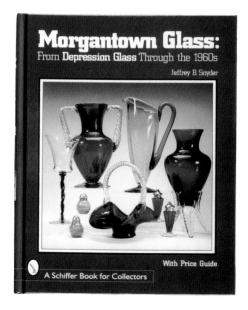

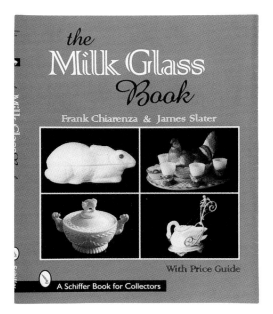

The Milk Glass Book Frank Chiarenza & James Slater. "Milk glass" today is considered neither white nor entirely opaque, as illustrated by more than 450 photos in this book. Drawn from the extensive collections of members of the National Milk Glass Collectors Society, most pieces pictured here have not appeared in any previous book. Even long-time collectors will be surprised to see items they have never encountered. American, English, French and other foreign manufacturers are represented. Some pieces are shown here in extremely rare colors. A special section shows items that have puzzled collectors or whose distinctive qualities merit special attention. Twenty-four pages from early catalogs of the French glasshouses Vallerysthal and Portieux are reprinted in color illustrating exquisite pieces. A checklist of major manufacturers, selected readings, index, and value guide are also provided. A must for lovers of milk glass, this book will appeal to all who appreciate finely-made glass.

Size: 8 1/2" x 11"   450+ color photos   228 pp.
Price Guide   Index
ISBN: 0-7643-0661-8   hard cover $49.95

Cobalt Blue Glass Monica Lynn Clements & Patricia Rosser Clements. Glass the color of deep blue, known as cobalt blue, holds a fascination for collectors of glassware. The origin of this distinctive blue glass goes back to the Egyptians. In Cobalt Blue Glass, authors Monica Lynn Clements and Patricia Rosser Clements showcase nearly 400 photographs that illustrate the wide appeal of cobalt blue glass. From Depression Era patterns and elegant glassware to reproduction pieces and new glass, the colorful photographs exemplify what appeals to the collector. Also shown are cobalt blue glass jewelry, condiment pieces, candlesticks, vases, lamps, bells, perfume bottles, bottles and jars, animals, iridescent glass pieces, and other items. This book contains current market values. For anyone who appreciates the beauty of cobalt blue glass, this book is an indispensable reference guide.

Size: 8 1/2" x 11"   391 color photos   144 pp.
Price Guide   Index
ISBN: 0-7643-0685-5   soft cover $24.95

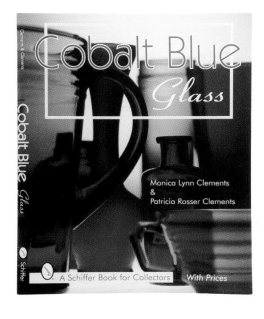

Royal Ruby Philip Hopper. *Royal Ruby* features 250 color photographs, 12 factory bulletins, and numerous catalog references to document Anchor Hocking's red glassware, which has fascinated collectors for years. First manufactured in the late 1930s, Anchor Hocking produced a multitude of Royal Ruby glassware items over the next fifty years. Many of the pieces in this book have never been included in any reference work, and some are experimental/test pieces never mass produced. Some of the more uncommon patterns detailed include High Point, Whirly Twirly, Fairfield, Classic, Berwick, Beverly, Shell, Fortune, and Rainflower. A detailed price guide, combined with a multitude of detailed photographs, make this a necessary reference for all Royal Ruby glass collectors.

Size: 8 1/2" x 11"   250 color photos   128 pp.
Price Guide
ISBN: 0-7643-0667-7   soft cover $24.95

Reflections on American Brilliant Cut Glass Bill & Louise Boggess. Valuable new information on American Brilliant Cut Glass is presented in the Boggesses' most recent work. Diverse sources including 135 originals catalogs, patent records, magazine advertisements and personal interviews with people within the glass industry as well as collectors and dealers were used to complete this thorough study. Patterns, colored patterns and their variations, common and unusual shapes, changing terminology, and signature marks are all discussed in detail. Rare pieces, such as those appearing in exhibitions, are also addressed. Over 950 photographs illustrate this comprehensive text.

Size: 8 1/2" x 11"   950 Photos   256 pp.
Price Guide
ISBN: 0-88740-722-6   hard cover $59.95

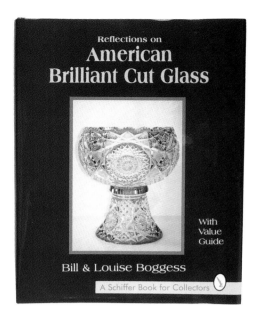

The Glass Industry in Sandwich, Volume Five Joan E. Kaiser & Raymond Barlow. This final volume contains 283 color photos of a variety of objects, from very fine cut and engraved ware to household, commercial, and scientific necessities that came under the heading of "general assortment" when they were marketed in the 1800's. A supplement to Volumes One, Two, Three and Four features objects that were not available for study at the time the books were written. A roster of 1500 employees and their occupations is included as an aid to documentation. There are still bargains to be had for as little as $10 as illustrated by the little-known or previously undocumented pieces pictured in this volume. Extremely rare articles have increased in value to as much as $35,000. Authorities Raymond E. Barlow and Joan E. Kaiser present to you a compendium of glass identifiable and collectible as Sandwich glass. A price guide is available that lists prices for each piece in clear and assorted colors, and updates the prices listed in previously published Barlow-Kaiser price guides.

Size: 9" x 12"   283 Photos   219 pp.
ISBN: 0-7643-0699-5   hard cover $79.95

Collecting Crackle Glass Judy Alford. This vibrantly colored and radiantly textured glass is captured in over 400 color photographs which show the history of yesteryear's spectacular crackle glass in detail. Collecting Crackle Glass is a book filled with valued information for collectors, dealers, and glassware lovers alike. The "manufacturer's identification" and "most collectible" guidelines make it easy to collect the most desirable pieces, and there is a value range for each piece of crackle glass photographed. Now you can have detailed information about the styles, shapes, colors, and crackling procedures needed to be able to pick up an unidentified piece of crackle glass and name its maker, know the approximate date of creation, and the fair market value. If you are a dealer, collector, or glassware lover, *Collecting Crackle Glass* is a book you will value and refer to time and time again.

Size: 8 1/2" x 11"   445 color photos   160 pp.
Price Guide
ISBN: 0-7643-0217-5   soft cover $29.95

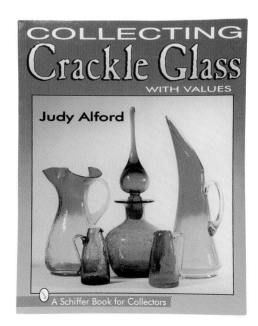

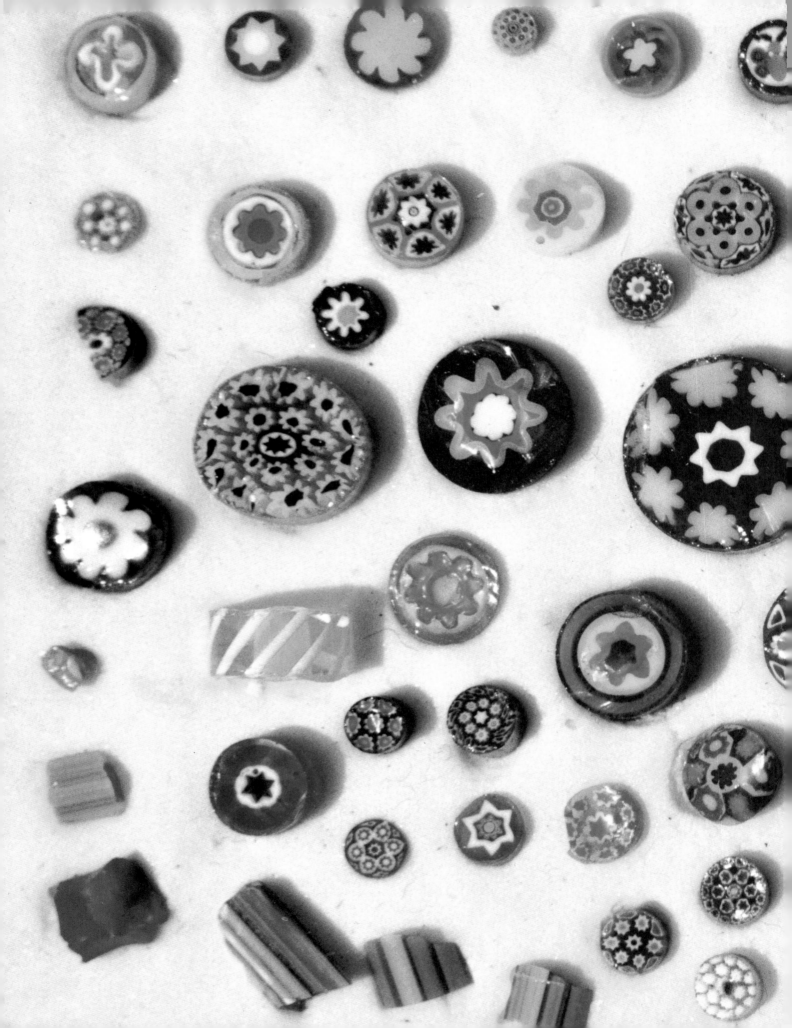